PHEROMONES, I:
Current Research

Papers by
D. L. Struble, H. H. Shorey, G. N.
Lanier et al.

MSS Information Corporation
655 Madison Avenue, New York, N. Y. 10021

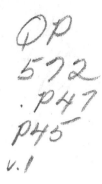

Library of Congress Cataloging in Publication Data

Main entry under title:

Pheromones: current research.

   1. Pheromones--Addresses, essays, lectures.
2. Insect hormones--Addresses, essays, lectures.
[DNLM: 1. Invertebrate hormones--Collected works.
2. Pheromones--Collected works. QL495 S927p]
QL495.P49   595.7'01'927   74-4250
ISBN 0-8422-7211-9 (Vol. 1)
ISBN 0-8422-7212-7 (Vol. 2)

TABLE OF CONTENTS

CREDITS AND ACKNOWLEDGEMENTS

Blum, M.S.; R.M. Crewe; W.E. Kerr; L.H. Keith; A.W. Garrison; and M. M. Walker, "Citral in Stingless Bees: Isolation and Functions in Trail-laying and Robbing," *Journal of Insect Physiology*, 1970, 16:1637-1648.

Coster, Jack E., "Production of Aggregating Pheromones in Re-emerged Parent Females of the Southern Pine Beetle," *Annals of the Entomological Society of America*, 1970, 63:1186-1187.

Green, N.; M. Jacobson; and J.C. Keller, "Hexalure, an Insect Sex Attractant Discovered by Empirical Screening," *Experientia*, 1969, 25:682.

Happ, George M., "Multiple Sex Pheromones of the Mealworm Beetle, *Tenebrio molitor* L.," *Nature*, 1969, 222:180-181.

Happ, George M.; Mark E. Schroeder; and James C.H. Wang, "Effects of Male and Female Scent on Reproductive Maturation in Young Female *Tenebrio molitor*," *Journal of Insect Physiology*, 1970, 16:1543-1548.

Henzell, R.F.; and M.D. Lowe, "Sex Attractant of the Grass Grub Beetle," *Science*, 1970, 168:1005-1006.

Jacobson, Martin, "Sex Pheromone of the Pink Bollworm Moth: Biological Masking by Its Geometrical Isomer," *Science*, 1969, 163:190-191.

Jacobson, Martin; Meyer Schwarz; and Rolland M. Waters, "Gypsy Moth Sex Attractants: A Reinvestigation," *Journal of Economic Entomology*, 1970, 63:943-945.

Jeanne, Robert L., "Chemical Defense of Brood by a Social Wasp," *Science*, 1970, 168:1465-1466.

Lanier, G.N., "Sex Pheromones: Abolition of Specificity in Hybrid Bark Beetles," *Science*, 1970, 169:71-72.

Menon, Maya, "Hormone-Pheromone Relationships in the Beetle, *Tenebrio molitor*," *Journal of Insect Physiology*, 1970, 16:1123-1139.

Menon, Maya; and K.K. Nair, "Sex Pheromone Production and Reproductive Behaviour in Gamma-Irradiated *Tenebrio molitor*," *Journal of Insect Physiology*, 1972, 18:1323-1331.

Nolte, D.J.; S.H. Eggers; and I.R. May, "A Locust Pheromone: Locustol," *Journal of Insect Physiology*, 1973, 19:1547-1554.

Nolte, D.J.; I.R. May; and B.M. Thomas, "The Gregarisation Pheromone of Locusts," *Chromosoma*, 1970, 29:462-473.

Riddiford, Lynn M.; and Carroll M. Williams, "Role of the Corpora Cardiaca in the Behavior of Saturniid Moths. I. Release of Sex Pheromone," *The Biological Bulletin*, 1971, 140:1-7.

Roelofs, W.L.; and A. Comeau, "Lepidopterous Sex Attractants Discovered by Field Screening Tests," *Journal of Economic Entomology*, 1970, 63:969-974.

Rudinsky, J.A.; and R.R. Michael, "Sound Production in Scolytidae: Chemostimulus of Sonic Signal by the Douglas-Fir Beetle," *Science*, 1972, 175:1386-1390.

Rudinsky, J.A.; V. Novák; and P. Švihra, "Pheromone and Terpene Attraction in the Bark Beetle *Ips typographus* L.," *Experientia*, 1971, 27:161-163.

Sanders, C.J., "Sex Pheromone Specificity and Taxonomy of Budworm Moths (Choristoneura)," *Science*, 1971, 171:911-913.

Shorey, H.H.; R.J. Bartell; and L.B. Barton Browne, "Sexual Stimulation of Males of *Lucilia cuprina* (Calliphoridae) and *Drosophila melanogaster* (Drosophilidae) by the Odors of Aggregation Sites," *Annals of the Entomological Society of America*, 1969, 62:1419-1421.

Sower, L.L.; H.H. Shorey; and Lyle K. Gaston, "Sex Pheromones of Noctuid Moths. XXI. Light:Dark Cycle Regulation and Light Inhibition of Sex Pheromone Release by Females of *Trichoplusia ni*," *Annals of the Entomological Society of America*, 1970, 63:1090-1092.

Strong, L., "Epidermis and Pheromone Production in Males of the Desert Locust," *Nature*, 1970, 228:285-286.

Struble, D.L.; and L.A. Jacobson, "A Sex Pheromone in the Red-backed Cutworm," *Journal of Economic Entomology*, 1970, 63:841-844.

PREFACE

Still largely mysterious, pheromones are the recently discovered compounds which serve to coordinate inter-individual behavior in many species of animals. Most pheromones thus far known are sexual and function as mate attractants in insects. They are extremely potent and have been successfully used for insect control. Insect pheromones also appear to control other aspects of behavior such as swarm aggregation. Recently sexual pheromones have been discovered in mammals, including primates. Their full role in regulation of mammalian behavior and physiology is still unknown.

This two-volume collection contains papers published in the period 1969 through early 1973. Volume I describes the existence, physiological function and biosynthesis of the best known pheromones, those of insects.

Volume II includes papers on the chemical analysis and synthesis of insect pheromones. The behavioral and physiological effects of pheromones in rodents as well as the biosynthesis of pheromones in rodents is described. Evidence for sexual pheromones in primates and other vertebrates is also presented.

Sex Pheromones of Insects

A Sex Pheromone in the Red-Backed Cutworm[1,2]

D. L. STRUBLE and L. A. JACOBSON

ABSTRACT

A sex pheromone was detected in females of *Euxoa ochrogaster* (Guenée). The method of extracting the pheromone and the olfactometer used for the laboratory bioassay are described. The sex pheromone was not extracted in detectable quantity from 4-day-old unmated females but was recovered in increasing concentrations from unmated females that were from 7 to 20 days old. The pheromone was recovered also from unmated and mated females that were collected in the field. Unmated males would not respond to the pheromone until they were 7 ± 2 days old and had been conditioned in the olfactometer for at least 2 days. The male response was greatest between 1.5 and 4 hours after the dark period began; at a temperature of $20\pm2°C$ they detected a minimum of 10^{-3} female equivalents of extract from 17- to 20-day-old females. The males survived in the olfactometers for an average of 23 days. Unmated males were stored at 5°C for up to 36 days after they emerged, with no diminution of their response to the pheromone.

Sex pheromones have been reported in many species of Lepidoptera (Jacobson 1965, Butler 1967), and the potential use of these pheromones for the detection and control of specific insect pests has been discussed by Jacobson (1965), Shorey et al (1968), and Regnier and Law (1968). This paper reports the presence of sex pheromone in females of the red-backed cutworm moth, *Euxoa ochrogaster* (Guenée),

---

[1] Lepidoptera: Noctuidae.
[2] Received for publication July 29, 1969.

11

a species of economic importance in western Canada and the United States. The conditioning of the moths, the extraction method, and the laboratory bioassay technique employed in detection of the pheromone are discussed.

MATERIALS AND METHODS.—The moths were obtained in 3 ways, by: rearing larvae collected in the field, collecting adults from the field, and rearing a culture in the laboratory. The larvae were reared individually by a method similar to that described by Jacobson and Blakeley (1957) for the pale western cutworm, *Agrotis orthogonia* Morrison. The pupae were sexed and placed singly in clean containers. The adults were placed in plastic cages containing pleated paper toweling for a resting surface and a vial of 10% honey solution as food. The males were stored in the dark at 5°C until they were used for the bioassay, and the females were stored under a prevailing diurnal cycle at 20±2°C.

The sex pheromone was extracted from the female moths by squeezing the abdomens with forceps to protrude the last 2 abdominal segments, which were then cut off. The portions of egg mass and hindgut that remained in the abdomen tips were removed. The amputated tips were thoroughly macerated in a mortar and extracted with 3 aliquots of purified methylene chloride (Vogel 1959). The combined extracts were filtered and concentrated to ca. 0.5 ml/ female abdomen tip on a rotary film evaporator at a pressure of 10 mm Hg at 0°C. The final solution was stored under nitrogen at −20°C to prevent oxidation of the crude extract.

The olfactometer (Fig. 1) used to bioassay the sex pheromone was a modification of that described by Gaston and Shorey (1964). Inexpensive cages were constructed from Plexiglas tubing (70 mm ID × 150 mm, Johnson Industrial Plastics (Western) Limited). One 90-mm-square endpiece was glued (with $CHCl_3$) to the cylinder, while the other detachable endpiece was held in position by 2 rubber bands as illustrated. A rubber fruit jar ring (Viceroy Manufacturing Co. Ltd.) provided an airtight seal between the end of the cylinder and the detachable end piece. A Pyrex glass air intake tube (25 mm OD × 125 mm) with a side arm (10 mm OD × 25 mm) was fitted with a 1-hole neoprene stopper into the fixed end of the olfactometer cage. A thermometer, a food container, and a glass exhaust tube (12 mm OD) were fitted into the detachable endpiece. The food container, made of Pyrex tubing (8 mm OD) with the inner end shaped to hold a piece of surgical gauze, could be filled with 10% honey solution without dismantling the olfactometer. The air-intake line was connected by rubber tubing (12 mm OD) to a pheromone-free air source. The air-exhaust line was similarly connected to an air-flow meter and a water aspirator. The water flow was adjusted to maintain an air flow of 1.5 to 2 liters/min per olfactometer.

Four olfactometers, with independent intake and exhaust lines, were assembled in a darkroom and positioned in front of a blue cardboard background that was illuminated by a red or white 7.5-w tungsten lamp. The intensity of the background light was controlled by a variable power supply and unless otherwise stated was set at 1.2–1.4 lux.

The sex pheromone was bioassayed in the following manner. Four unmated male moths were placed in each olfactometer cage, a 10% honey solution was continually available to the moths, and they were conditioned to a reverse diurnal cycle of 8 hr of darkness, beginning at 7 AM, and 16 hr of light using a 100-w bulb as the source. The olfactometer background light and air flow were left on continuously. The temperature within the olfactometer cages, unless otherwise stated, was $20\pm2°C$; the relative humidity was not controlled. At the desired testing time a known quantity, expressed in female equivalents (FE), of the crude pheromone extract was spotted on filter paper and introduced into the air-intake tube of the olfactometer by the method described by Gaston and Shorey (1964). The activity of the males was observed. When the test was completed the pheromone was removed and the moths were allowed to remain undisturbed for at least 24 hr before the tests were repeated.

RESULTS AND DISCUSSION.—We first detected the presence of a sex pheromone in the female moths by observing the responses of 8 unmated males (at least 12 days old) to an extract from 16 unmated females (aged 4–14 days). The sexual responses made by the resting males were similar to those described by Shorey et al. (1964) for the cabbage looper, *Trichoplusia ni* (Hübner). They included raising the antennae, vibrating the wings, flying toward the source of the pheromone, extending the claspers while wing vibrating or while flying, and attempting to copulate. Fig. 2 illustrates a typical resting male and 2 sexually aroused males. For bioassay purposes the response was considered positive when at least 50% of the males in an olfactometer either extended their claspers or attempted to copulate.

Our field observations led us to conclude that the maximum response by males to the pheromone probably occurs during the first 2–4 hr of darkness, as mating pairs were observed on the blossoms of cultivated sunflowers between 10.00 PM MST and midnight. For convenience of laboratory testing, unmated males were conditioned in the olfactometers to a reverse diurnal cycle. In the absence of pheromone, the males in the olfactometers were nonsexually active during the initial 1–1.5 hr of darkness and were usually in a resting position for the remainder of the dark period. Their best response to the pheromone was between 1.5 and 4 hr after the

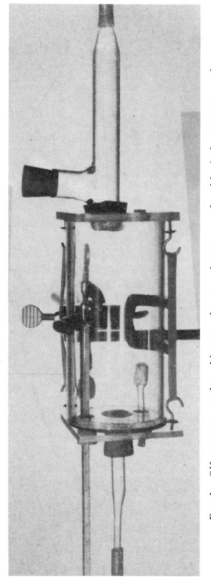

Fig. 1.—Olfactometer used to bioassay the sex pheromone of red-backed cutworm moths.

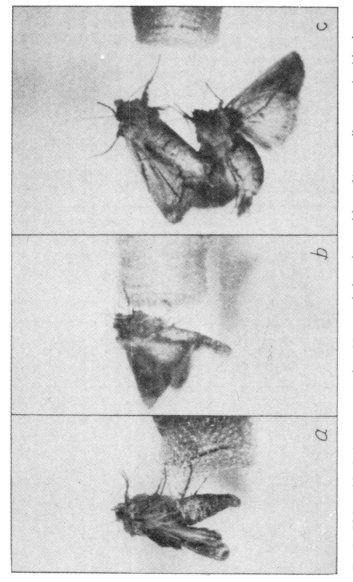

Fig. 2.—Male red-backed cutworm moths: (a) a typical resting position, (b) sexually aroused with claspers extended while vibrating the wings, (c) attempting to copulate. These were photographed in a light intensity of 1.2 lux with a 35-mm single-lens reflex camera equipped with an extended bellows, a short-mount 105-mm lens, and an electronic flash unit (1/2000-sec duration).

15

beginning of the dark period, which period corresponded to the time that mating was observed under natural conditions. The males responded sluggishly during the last 4 hr of darkness, and they would not respond during the light period.

The olfactometer background light intensity was varied from 0.3 (Gaston and Shorey 1964) to 350 lux. The moths responded well when the intensity was from 0.3 to 1.5 lux, but their response was very sluggish when the light intensity was greater than 22 lux. There was no difference in their response whether the background light was red or white.

The age at which the females possessed the maximum quantity of pheromone was established by extracting laboratory-reared unmated females of the following ages: 4, 6, 7, 11, 13, 17, and 20 days. These moths had been conditioned to the normal daily

Table 1.—The response of 28 conditioned males to the pheromone from female red-backed cutworm moths of various ages.

Females[a] extracted		Response of the males[b] to the pheromone extract at concentrations (FE) of[c]		
Age (days)	No.	10^{-1}	10^{-2}	10^{-3}
4	8	—	—	
6	8	—	—	
7	12	±	—	
11	8	+		
13	4	++		
17	4		++	++
20	4			+++
[d]	75 (unmated)			++
[d]	20 (mated)			++

[a] Prior to extraction the females were kept at room temperature under the normal daily cycle.
[b] The males were a minimum of 10 days old and had responded positively to 10^{-2} FE of pheromone extract from 14-day-old females. Each response is the avg of at least 4 tests.
[c] Symbols: — = no sexual response; ± = rubbing antennae and wing vibrating (response within 1–5 min); + = claspers were extended while wing vibrating or while flying (response within 1–5 min); ++ = same as (+) with attempted copulations (response within 1–3 min); +++ = same as (++) except response was within 30 sec.
[d] Females collected in the field, exact age unknown.

light cycle at room temperature. The various concentrations of the pheromone in the extracts were determined by observing the responses of 28 conditioned males. The results, summarized in Table 1, indicated that the pheromone was not present in detectable quantities until the females were about 7 days old, and the concentration increased with age at least up to 20 days. For the best pheromone recovery the females should be extracted when 17 to 20 days old, as under existing· conditions the

Table 2.—Conditioning of male red-backed cutworm moths in the olfactometers.

Lot	No. males	Age of moths (days) prior to			Conditioning prior to initial response (days)	Color background light bulb
		Conditioning	Initial response[a]	Death (avg)		
1	4	1	9	26	8	red
2	4	1	9	29	8	red
3	4	1	8	23	7	red
4	3	2	5	14	3	red
5	4	1	7	—[b]	6	white
6	4	2	6	21	4	white
7	3	2	5	24	3	white
8	4	2	8	—[b]	6	white
9	4	3	5	—[b]	2	white
10	2	5	7	24	2	white
		Mean 7±2		Mean 23		
11	4	9	11	27	2	red
12	4	30	33	41	3	red
13	4	19	21	36	2	red
14	5	32	33	43	1	red
15	4	36	37	45	1	white

[a] The initial positive response of males to 10^{-1} FE of extract from 11- to 17-day-old females.
[b] Moths were removed from the olfactometer before they died.

mortality increased rapidly beyond this age.

If an analogy can be made for the behavior of the moths between laboratory and natural conditions, our results indicate that the females probably do not mate in the field until they are about 7 days old. Because of this and the fact that multiple matings are common in the species (Jacobson 1970), there was a possibility that the pheromone could be recovered from a field population.

Females were collected in the field and conditioned in the laboratory for 7 days before the unmated and mated (some contained 7 spermatophores in the bursa copulatrix) moths were extracted separately. Conditioned males responded positively to 10^{-3} FE of extract from either the unmated or mated females. Therefore, it is possible to isolate the pheromone from the field population.

Throughout the tests the unmated males would not respond to the pheromone until they were 7±2 days old and had been conditioned in the olfactometer for at least 2 days (Table 2). The average lifetime of males that were placed in the olfactometers 1 to 5 days after they emerged was 23 days at 20±2°C. The males responded to the pheromone until they died. Conditioned males responded to the pheromone over a temperature range of 5–31°C.

However, at 5°C they reacted sluggishly, and at 31°C their average lifetime was expected to be much less than 23 days (Jacobson 1970). Unmated males that were stored in the dark at 5°C for 9–36 days responded to the pheromone after 1–3 days of conditioning in the olfactometer (Lot 11–14, Table 2). This method of prolonging the lifetime of the males did not appear to interfere with their olfactory response to the pheromone, indicating that unmated males can be used for bioassay for up to 36 days after emergence.

Our results indicate that neither males nor females mate under natural conditions until they are about 7 days old. It is also possible that males could remain practically dormant for up to 36 days during cool weather and still respond to the pheromone.

Pheromone extract is being accumulated for characterization of the active compound.

REFERENCES CITED

Butler, C. G. 1967. Insect pheromones. Biol. Rev. 42 (1) : 42–87.

Gaston, L. K., and H. H. Shorey. 1964. Sex pheromones of noctuid moths. IV. An apparatus for bioassaying the pheromones of six species. Ann. Entomol. Soc. Amer. 57 (6) : 779–80.

Jacobson, M. 1965. Insect Sex Attractants. Interscience Publishers, New York.

Jacobson, L. A. 1970. Laboratory ecology of the red-backed cutworm, Euxoa ochrogaster (Guenée) (Lepidoptera: Noctuidae). Can. Entomol. 102 (1) : 85–89.

Jacobson, L. A., and P. E. Blakeley. 1957. A method of rearing pale western cutworm, Agrotis orthogonia Morrison (Lepidoptera: Phalaenidae), in the laboratory. Can. Entomol. 89 (2) : 87–89.

Regnier, F. E., and J. H. Law. 1968. Insect pheromones. J. Lipid Res. 9 (5) : 541–51.

Shorey, H. H., L. K. Gaston, and T. R. Fukuto. 1964. Sex pheromones of noctuid moths. I. A quantitative bioassay for the sex pheromones of Trichoplusia ni (Lepidoptera: Noctuidae). J. Econ. Entomol. 57 (2) : 252–5.

Shorey, H. H., L. K. Gaston, and R. N. Jefferson. 1968. Insect sex pheromones, p. 57–127. In R. L. Metcalf [ed.] Advances in Pest Control Research. Interscience, New York.

Vogel, A. I. 1959. A Text Book of Practical Organic Chemistry. Longmans Green & Co. Ltd., London.

Sexual Stimulation of Males of *Lucilia cuprina* (Calliphoridae)[1] and *Drosophila melanogaster* (Drosophilidae)[1] by the Odors of Aggregation Sites

H.H. Shorey, R.J. Bartell, and L.B. Barton Browne

ABSTRACT

The level of sexual activity displayed by sexually mature males of *Lucilia cuprina* (Wiedemann) and *Drosophila melanogaster* Meigen (Diptera) increased when they were exposed to the odors of potential aggregation sites. The odorous source materials used were fresh sheep's liver and banana, respectively. The increased sexual activity for each species was similar to that obtained in response to the odors of conspecific females.

Females of *Lucilia cuprina* (Wiedemann) and *Drosophila melanogaster* Meigen are known to produce volatile sex pheromones that cause males of the respective species to increase their level of sexual activity. The most obvious component of sexual behavior exhibited by pheromone-stimulated males of

---

[1] Diptera.

L. cuprina is that of mounting nearby flies; this mounting is usually followed by genital contact and is a necessary precursor to the copulatory act (Bartell et al. 1969). Sexually active males of *D. melanogaster* exhibit an elaborate courtship behavior, with the basic behavioral element being a postural orientation toward a nearby fly. The frequency of occurrence of this orientation behavior is increased when the males are exposed to the female pheromone (Shorey and Bartell 1969). These elements of copulatory or courtship behavior will occur in all-male populations of either species, directed from one male to another. The following experiments were based on a comparison of the frequency at which the elements are directed toward other males in odorless air vs. air containing various odors.

In *L. cuprina* the odors of liver-fed flies were found to be more sexually stimulating to males than were those of nonliver-fed flies (Bartell et al. 1969). This finding suggested the possibility that some residual odor of liver possessed by the liver-fed flies may be important as a stimulus. Therefore, experiments were performed to examine the effect of the odor of liver alone on the sexual activity of *L. cuprina*. Because there is obvious biological significance in the possibility of sexual stimulation by odors arising from sites at which both sexes may aggregate, the investigations were extended to include a study of the responses of *D. melanogaster* males to the odor arising from ripe banana.

MATERIALS AND METHODS

The apparatus and method used for assaying odors with the 2 species is described elsewhere (Bartell et al. 1969, Shorey and Bartell 1969). A 2-way cock allowed clean air to pass either directly or by way of a chamber containing the odor source into a chamber containing 5 ♂. The odor source was placed in its chamber less than 15 sec before the air was directed through it, to prevent concentration of molecules in the stagnant air. Female flies to be used as an odor source were placed in the chamber in cages constructed of copper wire screen and polystyrene. Other odor sources—fresh sheep's liver, ripe banana, or water—were contained in aluminum vessels, with 3.2 cm^2 surface area of the source exposed to the air flow.

The assay males were exposed to a continuous flow of clean air for 3 min followed by a flow of odorous air for an additional 3 min. The males were observed continuously during this time for 2 components of behavior—locomotion and mounting other males for *L.*

cuprina (Bartell et al. 1969), and locomotion and orientation directed toward other males for *D. melanogaster* (Shorey and Bartell 1969). Locomotion recordings were based on direct counts of the number of flies in motion at the end of every 15-sec interval during the 6 min of assay. The responses to the various stimuli were expressed as a mean percentage occurrence of each designated behavioral act during the 3-min treatment phase (P) over the total occurrence during the full 6-min period of assay (3-min control phase (C) plus 3-min treatment phase). This percentage scale $[100P/(P+C)]$ was used because it is amenable to statistical analysis.

The assay flies were 3- to 6-day-old males which had not mated previously (either protein fed or nonprotein fed) and the odor-source females 3- to 6-day-old nonprotein-fed virgins. The sexes were isolated when they were less than 1 day old and were provided with sucrose and water only (nonprotein fed) or with sheep's liver (*L. cuprina*) or larval food medium (*D. melanogaster*) in addition (protein fed).

Experiments were conducted at a temperature of $24\pm2°C$, under ca. 300 lux illumination from fluorescent lamps. Each treatment was replicated 10–20 times.

RESULTS

Table 1 shows the responses of *L. cuprina* males. Significant ($P < 0.05$) increases in the sexual activity of either protein-fed or nonprotein-fed males of *L. cuprina* were elicited by the odors of both sheep's liver and females, whereas no appreciable effect was caused by water vapor. All treatments tended (without statistical significance in some cases) to cause small increases in locomotory activity by the assay males.

Table 1 shows the levels of responses of *D. melanogaster* males to odors from banana and 30 ♀. Both odorous treatments elicited significant increases in the number of orientations, whereas there was no significant effect of water vapor. Again, all treatments tended to cause small increases in locomotory activity.

DISCUSSION

Ripe banana was used to represent an odor source that will cause aggregation of both sexes of *D. melanogaster*. Also, banana is suitable as an adult feeding and oviposition site and a larval feeding medium for this species. Sheep liver fulfills these functions for *L. cuprina*, being used as an adult feeding and oviposition site and a larval feeding medium in our standard laboratory cultures of this insect.

The odor of the aggregation site materials caused significant increases in sexual activity of male flies of both species. This effect of odors was not attributable to water vapor evaporating from the sites. A water control used in the experiments with both species caused little or no increase in the frequency of male courtship or copulatory behavior. Also, the increased frequency of male courtship or copulatory behavior in response to odors arising from the aggregation site was not merely a reflection of an increase in locomotion by the stimulated males, since there appeared to be no consistent correlation between increases in the levels of locomotory activity and those of sexual activity (Table 1). This specificity of the sexual response produced by the aggregation site odor matches the specificity of response to the odor of conspecific females.

Even though increases in male locomotory activity for the 2 species appear to be sexually nonspecific.

Table 1.—Mean percentage frequency of response by males of 2 species of flies exposed to air bearing various odors, out of total frequency during equal control and exposure periods.

Feeding status of assay males	Odor source	Type of response ($\% \pm$ SE)	
Lucilia cuprina			
		Locomotion	Mounting
Protein fed	10 ♀	55.5±7.3	79.2±3.5[a]
	Liver	58.1±2.7[b]	77.4±5.1[a]
	Water	60.0±5.7	52.3±4.1
Protein fed	10 ♀	54.9±2.0[b]	71.1±4.5[a]
	Liver	57.6±1.4[a]	72.7±2.6[a]
	Water	55.6±1.6[a]	47.9±5.2
Drosophila melanogaster			
		Locomotion	Orientations
Protein fed	30 ♀	63.7±2.5[a]	84.9±1.2[a]
	Banana	62.6±2.3[a]	85.1±1.3[a]
	Water	54.6±2.1	53.1±2.3
Nonprotein fed	30 ♀	60.2±2.1[a]	87.8±2.9[a]
	Banana	63.4±1.7[a]	86.7±0.9[a]
	Water	58.8±2.1[a]	60.0±6.4

[a] $P <0.005$ for difference from 50%.
[b] $P <0.05$ for difference from 50%.

being stimulated by odors of aggregation sites and of females, they do enhance the likelihood of mating when both sexes are present, because they increase the probability that a male will come near a female. Then close range stimuli in addition to the odorous component, such as contact chemical stimuli received from the female, could operate to induce male courtship or copulatory behavior.

General Considerations.—Feeding and oviposition sites to which adults of both sexes are attracted probably serve as mating sites for many species of Diptera. Foster (1967) noted that various species of Diptera utilize freshly dropped cattle dung as a congregation site where mating occurs. Hammer (1941) reported on the congregation and mating at dung by flies of several species within 3 families of Diptera (Cordyluridae, Sepsidae, and Cypselidae). Males of *Orthellia lauta* (Wiedemann) (Muscidae) "lie in wait" around dung pads for the females' approach and mating takes place within a radius of 1–2 ft from the dung (P. Ferrar, personal communication). Laboratory observations on *L. cuprina* showed that males and females, even though protein fed, made frequent visits to a fresh liver. Both sexes were sexually unresponsive during the time in which tarsal contact with the liver was maintained, but males were highly active sexually in the immediate vicinity of the liver, and frequent matings took place within a few inches of the site. In our laboratory we have observed courtship and copulation between males and females of *D. melanogaster* that were attracted to and alighted on a small piece of banana. This effect of the site seems reasonable, because we assume that any factor that causes an aggregation of adults of both sexes will facilitate mating because of the increased random chance of a male encountering a female when the population density is raised. However, it is apparent that in addition to the passive role that the site plays in facilitating mating by providing a place where both sexes aggregate, it also may play an active role by providing odorous stimulation that lowers the threshold for release of courtship or copulatory behavior among the males.

It is interesting to speculate on the evolutionary significance of this phenomenon—that the odor of a female or of an aggregation site can stimulate male sexual behavior. In ancestral species of these flies and probably in many insect species today, the site may have acted passively only, causing bisexual aggregations, with the courtship and copulatory behavior of males being influenced by nonodorous stimuli produced by the females, such as sound, vision, or contact. Later, the odor of the aggregation site may have become, by a process of selection, a stimulus that lowered the threshold for release of male courtship or copulatory behavior, increasing the likelihood of males mating with nearby females. The evolution of new sensory mechanisms would not have been required, because the sensilla that respond to the odor of the site and lead to the orientation of the males to the site were already present. Finally, a pheromone produced by the females themselves would have had selective advantage, increasing the probability that males would attempt courtship or copulation with females, even in the absence of the aggregation site odor. Initially, this female sex pheromone may have been similar to the site odor, with later chemical and sensory evolution leading to a possible diversification of pheromones among various species. This suggested evolutionary sequence is similar to that proposed by Moore (1967) in his consideration of possible stages in the evolution of insect sex pheromones.

REFERENCES CITED

Bartell, R. J., H. H. Shorey, and L. Barton Browne. 1969. Pheromonal stimulation of the sexual activity of males of the sheep blowfly, *Lucilia cuprina* (Calliphoridae) by the female. Anim. Behav. (In press.)

Foster, W. A. 1967. Cooperation by male protection of ovipositing female in the Diptera. Nature (London) 214: 1035–6.

Hammer, O. 1941. Biological and ecological investigations on flies associated with pasturing cattle and their excrement. Vidensk. Medd. Naturhist Foren. Kjobenhavn 105: 1–257.

Moore, B. P. 1967. Chemical communication in insects. Science J. 3: 44–49.

Shorey, H. H., and R. J. Bartell. 1969. Role of a female sex pheromone in stimulating male courtship behaviour in *Drosophila melanogaster*. Anim. Behav. (In press.)

Sex Pheromones: Abolition of Specificity in Hybrid Bark Beetles

G. N. LANIER

Abstract. *Specificity of sex pheromones maintains breeding isolation among three closely related species of spruce-infesting* Ips. *Hybrids produced in the laboratory were intermediate to the parent species in both attractiveness and response. Pheromones and pheromone receptor types in the hybrids are probably mixtures of those of the parent species.*

The spruce-infesting bark beetles (Scolytidae) *Ips amiskwiensis* G. Hopping and *I. borealis* (Eichhoff) are sympatric along the eastern edge of the Canadian Rockies (*1*). Near Banff, Alberta, these species commonly infest the same host tree, but I have been unable to find them inhabiting the same gallery systems. *Ips pilifrons* Swaine infests spruce in the southern Rocky Mountains and meets *I. amiskwiensis* in the vicinity of the Grand Tetons, Wyoming (*2*).

Although *I. amiskwiensis* will produce fertile hybrids with *I. borealis* and *I. pilifrons* in forced laboratory pairings, putative hybrids are rare in nature. Introgression is presumably averted by specificity of sex pheromones (*3*). I have found support for this hypothesis in field and laboratory tests of females' responses to pheromones produced by various pure and hybrid males. The same tests indicate that hybrids produce a mixture of pheromones and inherit pheromone receptor types of both parent species.

For each laboratory test, 36 males (12 each of three kinds) were induced to bore into a freshly cut spruce bolt (*4*) in a 6 by 6 Latin square design. Each kind of male was represented twice in every row and column. After males were allowed 2 days to excavate nuptial chambers, 72 females of one kind (occasionally less than 72 were available) were released on the infested bolt in a cage made by joining two 1-gallon Sealright (*5*) food cartons. Four days later the bark was carefully stripped from the log and the number of females in, or constructing egg galleries from, each nuptial chamber was recorded. Nuptial chambers rather than males were considered in the assessment of the relative attractiveness of the kinds tested; occasionally males failed to become established, whereas others abandoned the initial nuptial chamber to construct a second. Correct identification of such males was assured by prior marking of each kind with a different lacquer.

In the first type of field test, small

25

logs, each previously infested with five males of one kind, were placed 5 m apart in a Latin square. Each kind appeared once in every row and column. After 10 days, results were assessed as in laboratory tests. In the second type of field test, logs, each containing 40 males of one kind, were placed in individual greenhouse cages and responding beetles were collected in a tray of water under a window trap (6).

In 56 of 57 laboratory tests, more pure females responded to males of their own species than to males of other species. Based on attraction to males of its own kind as index 100, attraction indices (7) for *I. amiskwiensis* females to *I. pilifrons* and *I. borealis* were 37 and 19, respectively (Table 1). Indices for reciprocal tests were 11 and 15. In field tests, *I. amiskwiensis* was very slightly, if at all, attracted to other species (Table 2).

Pure females generally responded to hybrid males at a level intermediate to the response to males of the parent species. Attraction indices for *I. pilifrons* and *I. borealis*—to the pure species and their F_1 and B_1 progeny with *I. amiskwiensis*—are clearly in the same order as their blood relationships. For example, the responses of female *I. pilifrons* to male *pilifrons*, B_1 p $(a$-$p)$ (8), F_1 a-p, B_1 a $(a$-$p)$, and *I. amiskwiensis* were 100, 35, 27, 13, and 11, respectively (Table 1). *Ips amiskwiensis* females also responded in order of blood relationship with *I. borealis* and backcrosses in both laboratory (Table 1) and field tests (Table 2, test 1). However, the ability of *I. amiskwiensis* to discriminate apparently broke down in laboratory tests invo'ving its F_1 hybrid with *I. pilifrons*. Furthermore, it did not differentiate between the B_1 p $(a$-$p)$ and a $(a$-$p)$ in the laboratory or in the field (Table 2, tests 2 and 3).

Hybrid a-p females were slightly more attracted to males of their own kind than to those of the two parent species (Table 1). Backcross p $(a$-$p)$ and a $(a$-$p)$ females were attracted strongly to males of the backcross spe-

Table 1. Attraction indices (8) and number of tests (italics) for *Ips amiskwiensis* (*a*), *I. pilifrons* (*p*), *I. borealis* (*b*), and F_1 and backcross (B_1) hybrids, determined in the laboratory. NT, not tested.

Females	Male pheromone				
	a	*a* (*a-p*)	*a-p*	*p* (*a-p*)	*p*
I. amiskwiensis	100-*8*	52-*2*	63-*4*	59-*2*	37-*8*
B_1 *a* (*a-p*)	189-*4*	100-*4*			82-*4*
F_1 *a-p*	78-*4*		100-*4*		89-*4*
B_1 *p* (*a-p*)	30-*4*			100-*4*	143-*4*
I. pilifrons	11-*8*	13-*4*	27-*3*	35-*5*	100-*10*
	a	*a* (*a-b*)	*a-b**	*b* (*a-b*)	*b*
I. amiskwiensis	100-*6*	42-*4*	NT	34-*3*	19-*5*
B_1 *a* (*a-b*)	94-*8*	100-*8*	NT		47-*8*
B_1 *b* (*a-b*)	52-*5*		NT	100-*5*	115-*5*
I. borealis	15-*5*	19-*5*	NT	74-*4*	100-*7*

Table 2. Attraction indices (8) of female *Ips amiskwiensis* to various pure and hybrid males determined in the field. Tests 1 and 2, females taken from nuptial chambers of males; test 3, females captured in traps. NT, not tested.

Test	Total taken (No.)	Male pheromone							
		p	p (a-p)	a-p	a (a-p)	a	a (a-b)	b (a-b)	b
1	71	10	15	66	NT	100	NT	21	9
2	90	0	46	45	39	100	37	1	0
3	100	16	69	NT	66	100	62	0	NT

cies, less to males of their own kind, and least to males of the other parental species. F_1 *a-b* were insufficient in number for inclusion in tests. Backcross female *b* (*a-b*) responded in the manner just described. However, the *a* (*a-b*) females were attracted nearly equally to males of the same kind and to *I. amiskwiensis*.

From these tests it is clear that specificity of sex pheromones tends to prevent natural hybridization between *I. amiskwiensis* and *I. borealis* or *I. pilifrons*. Comparisons of laboratory and field tests with *I. amiskwiensis* suggest that specificity is greatest under field conditions and that greater discrimination is exercised in entering nuptial chambers (log tests) than in flying to the attractant (trap tests). However, natural hybrids which might occur could readily breed among themselves, or assimilate with either parent species.

Pheromones and pheromone receptors of hybrids theoretically could be new, the same as those of the parent species (either singly or in combination), or a combination of new and parent types. Receptors of pheromones in some insects have been shown to be quite specific; even isomers of the same compound often fail to evoke equivalent response (9). It is therefore unlikely that the genetic condition of hybrids results in new receptors which are spontaneously keyed to new pheromones. Rather, the parent pheromones and receptors are probably present in proportions similar to the degree of het-

erosis. If the olfactory response is a function of the number of individual receptors stimulated (10), the F_1 *a-p* females should be expected to respond highest to F_1 *a-p* males because the mixed pheromones of those males would excite the maximum number of the mixed receptors of the females. The preference of backcross females for the pheromone of the pure (backcross) species would also be predicted (11). Lack of discrimination by *I. amiskwiensis* between pheromones produced by male *p* (*a-p*) and *a* (*a-p*) and the partial breakdown in response specificity of this species in the presence of the F_1 *a-p* pheromone may be associated phenomena—the cause of which could come to light when the chemistry of the component pheromones is known.

References and Notes

1. G. R. Hopping, *Can. Entomol.* **97**, 159 (1965); *ibid.*, p. 193.
2. Based on recent collections by the author.
3. The male *Ips* selects the host tree, initiates the attack, and constructs a nuptial chamber in the phloem-cambium region. In so doing it discharges a pheromone which attracts both sexes, stimulates mass attack on the host selected, and induces females to enter the nuptial chambers and mate [R. F. Anderson, *J. Econ. Entomol.* **41**, 596 (1948); D. L. Wood and J. P. Vité, *Contrib. Boyce Thompson Inst.* **21**, 79 (1961)]. Cross attractiveness of sex pheromones has been demonstrated for several closely related allopatric bark beetles [J. P. Vité, R. I. Gara, H. D. von Scheller, *ibid.* **22**, 461 (1964); D. L. Wood and G. N. Lanier, unpublished data]. However, sympatric species are generally not cross attractive [R. C. Wilkinson, *Fla. Entomol.* **47**, 57 (1964);

J. P. Vité, *Naturwissenschaften* **52**, 267 (1965)].

4. *Picea engelmannii*, 40 cm long and 10 to 20 cm in diameter.
5. Crown Zellerbach Ltd.
6. J. A. Chapman, *Can. Entomol.* **98**, 50 (1966); —— and J. M. Kinghorn, *ibid.* **87**, 46 (1955).
7. Attraction index of *b* to *a*, for example, is calculated as follows: *b* per *a* nuptial chamber divided by *a* per *a* nuptial chamber times 100.
8. *I. amiskwiensis, a; I. pilifrons, p; I. borealis, b*; the progeny resulting from backcross (B_1) of *I. amiskwiensis–I. pilifrons* hybrids to *I. pilifrons* are designated *p (a-p)*.
9. M. Jacobson, *Insect Sex Attractants* (Interscience, New York, 1967).
10. D. Schneider, *J. Insect Physiol.* **8**, 15 (1962).
11. The simplest genetic situation possible is single loci for pheromone and pheromone receptor type. Thus, the genotype for receptors of the F_1 *amiskwiensis-pilifrons* would be *ap* and those of the backcross to *pilifrons* would be ½ *ap* and ½ *pp*. The response of backcross females with the *ap* genotype is expected to be similar to that of the F_1. Those with the *pp* genotype should respond in a manner similar to *I. pilifrons*. If the response levels of the two genotypes predicted by the attraction indices in Table 1 are summed, it is clear that the *I. pilifrons* pheromone will provide the greatest aggregate attraction to backcross females. If more than one locus is responsible for determining receptor type, this preference of the B_1 to the backcross species should be accentuated. These approximations could be further complicated if more than one compound differs in the respective pheromones. The sex pheromone of *Ips confusus* (LeConte) consists of three compounds which act synergistically [R. M. Silverstein, J. O. Rodin, D. L. Wood, *Science* **154**, 509 (1966); D. L. Wood, R. W. Stark, R. M. Silverstein, J. O. Rodin, *Nature* **215**, 206 (1967)]. *Ips latidens* (LeConte), a primitive species in my judgment, was attracted to a combination of two of these compounds, but response was inhibited by addition of the third compound [D. L. Wood *et al.*, cited above].
12. I thank Dr. J. A. Chapman for review of the manuscript and G. A. Shofer for technical assistance.

Sex Attractant of the Grass Grub Beetle

R. F. HENZELL, M. D. LOWE

Abstract. *The sex attractant produced by adult females of the grass grub beetle* Costelytra zealandica *(White) has been isolated and identified as phenol. Field tests with phenol-water mixtures were attractive to male beetles in particular.*

We report phenol, which has been isolated from the female beetle of *Costelytra zealandica* (White) (Scarabaeidae: Coleoptera), as a sex attractant for the male beetle of the same species. The larval stage of this insect pest is of major economic importance in New Zealand, causing considerable pasture damage.

Evidence for the presence of a chemical sex attractant in the female beetle has been described by Henzell *et al.* (*1*). The attractant was isolated from 1500 virgin female beetles by washing their abdomens with diethyl ether. The ether extract was concentrated to 0.5 ml by rotary evaporation at 25°C and 70 mm-Hg, and then sublimed on to a condenser cooled with Dry Ice, in a short-path apparatus at 30°C and 0.001 mm-Hg for 3 hours. The biologically active sublimate in diethyl ether was chromatographed (by spotting) on silica gel plates and eluted with two systems, chloroform and 10 percent ether in hexane. Only one active area, whose R_F value was consistent with that of phenol, was obtained with each system. A similar result was obtained when the extract was chromatographed on Whatman No. 1 filter paper and eluted with water, ethyl alcohol, or a mixture (1 : 1) of diethyl ether and ethyl alcohol.

The active sublimate was dissolved in diethyl ether and examined by preparative gas-liquid chromotography with five different column packings: 10 percent Carbowax 20M on 60-80 mesh Gas Chrome P; 4 percent UCW98 on 60-80 mesh Gas Chrome P; 2 percent Apiezon L on 60-80 mesh Silocel; 2 percent DEGS on 60-80 mesh Gas

Chrome Z; 2 percent Altox G-1292 on 40-70 mesh Silocel.

Fractions were collected from each of the columns and bioassayed. An active fraction was obtained only from the 2 percent Atlox G-1292 column. The active compound, approximately 130 μg, had a retention time of 5.2 minutes which corresponded precisely with that of phenol. This collected fraction was dissolved in diethyl ether and examined by mass spectroscopy. Its spectrum was consistent with that of a mixture of phenol in diethyl ether, and the presence of phenol was confirmed by measuring the masses of the ions at (mass to charge) m/e 94, 66, 65, and 39. These had the expected compositions of C_6H_6O, C_5H_6, C_5H_5, and C_3H_3. In addition it was established by use of the "defocusing" technique that the following transitions had taken place; $94 \rightarrow 66$, $93 \rightarrow 65$, $66 \rightarrow 65$, and $65 \rightarrow 39$. There was no evidence that the ion $C_6H_6O^+$ had arisen from a precursor of higher molecular weight; therefore it can be confidently concluded that the compound under examination was phenol.

Laboratory bioassay was carried out as described (1), except that each fraction was placed on a paraffin dummy which was then dropped among ten male beetles confined under an inverted filter funnel (12 cm in diameter). Beetles responded within a few minutes to dummies treated with 0.1, 1.0, and 10.0 μg, respectively, of pure phenol, by attempting to copulate with the dummies as well as with one another. Eighty percent of the males responded to each amount of phenol on the dummy. Analysis by gas-liquid chromatography (2) of ethereal extracts of female abdomens indicated that each beetle contains between 0.5 and 1.0 μg of phenol, which corresponds to approximately 10 to 20 parts per million by weight. No phenol was detected in ethereal extracts of male abdomens.

Field tests were carried out to examine the attractiveness of phenol. Pure phenol mixed with water at concentrations varying from 500 to 10 ppm were attractive to the male beetle in particular. Two liters of the phenol-water mixtures was placed in open tins and tested at dusk when beetle flights occurred. On one such evening a total of 71 males and no females were caught in seven traps each containing approximately 100 ppm of the phenol-water mixture. On the following evening 222 males and 19 females were caught in the same traps. Control traps containing water and placed alongside each baited trap did not catch any beetles.

Reports on insect sex attractants have revealed structural characteristics that allow the attractants to be classified into three major groups: unsaturated alcohols and their esters, aliphatic acids, and terpene-like compounds (3). Phenol obviously does not fit into any of these groups. In fact, to our knowledge, while phenol occurs in plants (4), its presence has never been reported in insects.

References and Notes

1. R. F. Henzell, M. D. Lowe, H. J. Taylor, E. Boston, *New Zealand J. Sci.* **12**, 252 (1969).
2. The gas chromatography was carried out on an F and M model 402 instrument equipped with dual flame-ionization detectors. Preparative gas-liquid chromatography was carried out with a glass U tube (1.5 m by 14 mm) of 2 percent Atlox G1292 on 40-70 mesh Silocel at 120°C; the nitrogen carrier flow was 40 cm³/min.
3. Yu. B. Pyatnova, L. L. Ivanov, A. S. Kyskina, *Russ. Chem. Rev. Engl. Transl.* **38**, 126 (1969).
4. W. Karrer, *Konstitution und Vorkommen der organischen Pflanzenstoffe* (Birkhauser AG, Basel, 1958), p. 72.
5. We thank Dr. R. Hodges of Massey University for his mass spectral analysis and Dr. E. P. White of this Centre for advice and constructive criticism during this project.

Sex Pheromone Specificity and Taxonomy of Budworm Moths (Choristoneura)

C. J. SANDERS

Abstract. *Of six closely related species of budworm moths, three share the same or similar sex pheromones. Two of the others share another sex pheromone, but are geographically isolated. The sixth species, which is the most morphologically distinct, shows only slight affinity to the others.*

The genus *Choristoneura* of the lepidopterous family Tortricidae includes a group of coniferous defoliators which are of considerable economic importance in both western and eastern North America. Six of the presently recognized species were included in the single species *C. fumiferana* (Clem.) until 1953 when Freeman (*1*) described *C. pinus* Free., the jack-pine budworm, as a distinct species, a view supported by subsequent field observations (*2*). In 1967, *C. fumiferana* was further subdivided (*3*). The name *C. fumiferana* was restricted to the eastern spruce budworm of the boreal forests and the western populations were divided into four new species. These were *C. occidentalis* Free., the western 1-year-cycle budworm, ranging from British Columbia to New Mexico; *C. biennis*

Free., the western 2-year-cycle budworm, of the mountains of British Columbia and Alberta with adults appearing in the even numbered years only; *C. orae* Free., the coastal budworm, from the coast of British Columbia; and *C. viridis* Free., the green budworm, from Oregon and California. Separation was based largely on differences in the frequencies of polymorphic traits as well as on differences in physiology, geographic range, and host preference. Reliable distinguishing characters could not be found in the male or female genitalia, and indeed the species will hybridize in the laboratory, although mating is not indiscriminate.

When these species were described, the importance of sex pheromones in mating behavior was not ap-

31

Table 1. Response of males of six species of *Choristoneura* to female sex pheromones in laboratory bioassays.

Females	Males responding (%)					
	C. fumi- ferana	C. occi- dentalis	C. biennis	C. orae	C. viridis	C. pinus
C. fumiferana	53	42	60	0	0	0
C. occidentalis	25	40				
C. biennis	0		5			
C. orae	2			36	0	20
C. viridis	0			0	0 (24)*	16
C. pinus	0	0		30	0	19

* Response to crushed tip of female abdomen.

preciated. Subsequently Roelofs and Comeau (4) have demonstrated the value of sex pheromone specificity in taxonomic studies, and I have previously reported the specificity of the sex pheromones of the two sympatric eastern species, *C. fumiferana* and *C. pinus* (5). I now report studies on the relationships among the sex pheromones of the other four species.

Collections of larvae and pupae of the four western species and *C. pinus* were obtained during June and July 1970 with the cooperation of personnel from the USDA Forest Service and the Canadian Forestry Service. Larvae were reared to maturity on their native host plant where available, or on eastern white spruce and balsam fir. After pupation the insects were sexed; adult males were kept for bioassays, females for the collection of pheromone and for field trials of their attractancy. Adult *C. fumiferana* were available throughout the experiments from field collections and laboratory-reared stock.

Solutions containing the sex pheromones were obtained by leaving groups of females in 1000-ml flasks for one or more nights and then rinsing out the flasks with ether (previous experiments with *C. fumiferana* had shown

that extracts obtained by the more conventional means of cutting off the tips of the females' abdomens were biologically inactive). The resulting washes were made up to a concentration of one female-night per milliliter; that is, a wash from 100 females left for two nights would be made up to 200 ml. Bioassays were conducted by expelling air from a medicine dropper that had previously been used to suck up approximately 0.5 ml of the pheromone solution into plastic boxes containing males. Buzzing by the males (circling on the substrate with rapidly beating wings) was considered a positive response (5).

The results (Table 1) show that both *C. occidentalis* and *C. biennis* males responded to *C. fumiferana* washes whereas *C. fumiferana* males responded to *C. occidentalis* washes, though at a lower level than their response to washes from *C. fumiferana* females. Inexplicably, washes from *C. biennis* females were not biologically active. Neither *C. orae* nor *C. viridis* males responded to *C. fumiferana* washes; however, *C. orae* and *C. pinus* males responded equally well to washes of their own or each others' females. *C. viridis* washes produced no response

32

Table 2. Numbers of male *C. fumiferana* and *C. pinus* field-trapped by virgin females of six species of *Choristoneura*. The total number of traps involved (each containing one female) and the total number of males caught are included to indicate the reliability of the data. The relative catch is expressed as the percentage of the numbers caught by *C. fumiferana* and *C. pinus* females, respectively.

Females	*C. fumiferana* males			*C. pinus* males		
	Relative catches	Traps (No.)	Total caught (No.)	Relative catches	Traps (No.)	Total caught (No.)
C. fumiferana	100	61	1163	1	3	10
C. occidentalis	53	17	181			
C. biennis	64	18	293			
C. orae	0	3	3	18	3	95
C. viridis	0	6	0	4	4	15
C. pinus				100	7	895
Controls (no female)		21	13		7	7

from *C. viridis* males, nor from *C. fumiferana* or *C. orae* males. However, they did evoke a response from *C. pinus* males, and *C. viridis* males did respond when presented with the tip of the abdomen of a female *C. viridis* crushed on filter paper.

These results were supplemented by field experiments in which virgin females were used to trap males in outbreaks of the two eastern species (*C. fumiferana* and *C. pinus*) to determine their attractancy to the native males. Single females were housed in screen cages placed in the center of plywood boards 1 foot square, coated with Stickem Special (Michel and Pelton Co., Emeryville, California) which trapped the attracted males. In each experiment the numbers of traps baited with test females or with native females were equal. Control traps containing no females were set up in each experiment, and the number of males caught on the controls was deducted from the numbers on the baited traps. The traps were left for three or four nights in each experiment. Variations in the density of the male populations led to differences in the number of males available for trapping in each experiment. The catches have, therefore, been stan-

dardized by expressing them as percentages of the number of males caught by the native females in each experiment (Table 2).

The results indicate that *C. fumiferana*, *C. occidentalis*, and *C. biennis* share the same or similar sex pheromones, whereas *C. pinus* and *C. orae* share a pheromone distinct from the first group. The laboratory tests with *C. viridis* were inconclusive, but suggest some affinity between *C. viridis* and *C. pinus*. However, in the field trials *C. viridis* females competed only poorly with *C. pinus* females, indicating that the affinity is not strong. This, coupled with the distinctive coloration of *C. viridis* larvae and adults, suggests that the relationship between *C. pinus* and *C. viridis* is not as close as the relationships among the other species.

Although strong interspecific attractancy was demonstrated within the two groups, in no case did the attractancy of the alien females equal that of the native females. This suggests that there are subtle differences in the pheromones themselves or in the manner of their release. Observations on the females showed that in all species, calling (extrusion of the sex pheromone gland) began before or shortly after dusk, which coincides with the peak activity of both *C. fumiferana* and *C. pinus* males (5). Therefore, the timing of the sex pheromone release is unlikely to be an important factor. Possibly the actual quantities of pheromone released by the females differ with the species, but it is also possible that secondary chemicals are involved that increase the specificity of the sex pheromones of each species as has been suggested by Roelofs and Tette (6).

The apparent affinity between *C. orae* and *C. pinus* is surprising, for *C. orae* is more similar in polymorphic characters to the group of *C. fumiferana, C. occidentalis,* and *C. biennis.* Furthermore, *C. orae* feeds on spruce and fir, whereas *C. pinus* feeds on pine, a dichotomy that has been accepted as a natural taxonomic division in the genus *Choristoneura.* The morphological differences between *C. orae* and *C. pinus* and the difference in sex pheromone between *C. orae* and the other western species confirm that *C. orae* is a valid species. Conceivably *C. orae, C. pinus,* and, possibly, *C. viridis* arose from a common ancestor and diverged through allopatric evolution; but the similarity of the sex pheromones among eastern and western species may be an example of parallel evolution, *C. orae,*

C. biennis, and *C. occidentalis* evolving as sibling species in the west, *C. pinus* and *C. fumiferana* as sibling species in the east.

The fact that *C. fumiferana, C. occidentalis,* and *C. biennis* all have the same or very similar pheromones raises questions concerning their relationship and possible isolating mechanisms. The range of the three species is not clearly defined at present, and there may be areas of contact. However, the potential for hybridization is reduced by ecological and temporal isolation and possibly also by the presence of secondary chemicals in the sex pheromones. The true relationship of these species will have to await detailed studies in the areas of potential contact.

References

1. T. N. Freeman, *Can. Entomol.* 85, 121 (1953).
2. S. G. Smith, *ibid.,* p. 141; *Evolution* 8, 206 (1954).
3. T. N. Freeman, *Can. Entomol.* 99, 449 (1967); G. Stehr, *ibid.,* p. 456; G. T. Harvey and G. Stehr, *ibid.,* p. 464; I. M. Campbell, *ibid.,* p. 482; G. T. Harvey, *ibid.,* p. 486.
4. W. L. Roelofs and A. Comeau, *Science* 165, 398 (1969).
5. C. J. Sanders, *Can. Entomol.,* in press.
6. W. L. Roelofs and J. P. Tette, *Nature* 226, 1172 (1970).

Pheromone and Terpene Attraction in the Bark Beetle *Ips typographus* L.

J. A. RUDINSKY, V. NOVÁK
and P. ŠVIHRA

We report the first evidence that *Ips typographus* L. (Coleoptera: Scolytidae) is strongly attracted to both certain terpenes and a pheromone produced by the male beetle. *Ips typographus* is the most destructive bark beetle in the extensive Norway spruce (*Picea excelsa* Link.) forests in Europe and Asia. The attraction seen in our field studies is similar to the olfactory mechanism which has been intensively studied in several North American scolytids, certain of which are already being experimentally manipulated with terpenes and synthesized pheromones[1, 2]. Therefore, further study is indicated of possible control of *I. typographus* by such means.

Earlier, male-produced pheromones were found in destructive *Ips* spp. on pines in North America[3] and in *I. acuminatus* Gyll. on pine in Norway[4]. MERKER[5], CHARARAS[6], ADLUNG[7] et al. have studied effects of host volatiles on *I. typographus* without relation to a pheromone.

The present study was made in 100-year-old spruce forests near Třeboň, Bohemia and Hronec, Slovakia, in May and June 1970. We separated and introduced mature males and females to sections of spruce logs 70 cm long placed in plastic-screened cages, $50 \times 50 \times 80$ cm. As controls we used naturally invaded log sections 2 days after attack, and uninvaded logs. The cages were

Response of *Ips typographus* to spruce logs invaded separately by males, females and pairs, and to 4 monoterpenes near Třeboň, Bohemia in May 1970 at 17–27°C

Materials tested	No. of beetles attracted						
	May 15	May 16	May 17	May 18	May 19	May 20	Total
A Log with males (27 entries)	52	52	16	39	34	17	210
B Log with females (4 entries)	1	3	0	1	3	1	9
C Log with pairs (13 entries)	2	7	4	6	16	8	43
D Naturally invaded log (80 entries)	182	232	181	254	297	76	1222
E Uninvaded log	2	3	2	1	0	2	10
F α-pinene[a]	2	1	19	23	38	7	90
β-pinene[a]	2	2	4	14	7	0	29
Limonene[a]	0	6	3	11	11	5	36
Camphene[a]	0	0	1	8	4	1	14

[a] In 1% ethanol solution.

36

placed 10–15 m apart in a forest opening of about 1 acre, and the attracted beetles alighting on the cages were collected at 10 min intervals. To test for the primary or host attraction known to be operative in other scolytids with secondary or insect-produced attraction[3, 8, 9], we used both natural log sections and 1% solutions of 4 terpene hydrocarbons in ethanol[10].

As it is practically impossible to separate the sexes of *I. typographus* by external morphological characters, we distinguished living beetles by their different boring behavior and location in the gallery. Males, which are known to initiate boring and construct the nuptial chamber before the females reach them, were collected in naturally infested trees as they started boring in the nuptial chamber. The females were taken in partly constructed egg galleries branching from the nuptial chambers. Following the experiment we debarked the logs and confirmed the sex separation by dissection (with virtually 100% accuracy). The sex of the attracted beetles was determined by dissection.

The response of flying beetles to the variously treated logs is shown in the Table. The attraction to the log with introduced males (Table A) is clear, and may be considered strong because of the disturbance of the test males' normal invasion process inherent to the method of collecting males to be introduced to the test logs. Not surprisingly, the naturally invaded log with undisturbed males (Table D) showed the greatest attractiveness. The ratio of male entry holes to attracted beetles in the naturally invaded log was 1:14, and in the log with disturbed males 1:7. It is evident from the response of flying beetles that the sexually mature male *I. typographus* produces the pheromone after entering the host.

Similar attraction occurred during the second flight of *I. typographus* in experiments performed near Hronec, Slovakia, 9–14 June 1970, with comparable numbers of beetles responding. Others tests, particularly of the sex ratio of attracted beetles, suggest the presence also of a factor regulating the mating behavior of the beetles aggregated on or near a host tree[11].

As expected, the pheromone attraction was numerically much greater than the response to terpenes. Table F shows that 3 terpenes were more attractive than the natural log, especially α-pinene. The sex ratio of attracted beetles (1 male : 1 female in a natural population of 1 male : 2–3 females) reflects the behavior of this species in that the host-selecting or guiding sex responds in greater numbers than the guided sex of this polygamous species.

It is interesting that 3 common predators of *I. typographus*, *Thanasimus formicarius* L. (Cleridae); *Medetera signaticornis* Lw. (Dolichopodidae); and *Epuraea pygmaea* Gyll. (Nitidulidae), also responded to both the terpenes and the male-invaded logs, suggesting that they may find their prey by this attraction mechanism.

I. typographus is known to prefer wind thrown, damaged or weakened trees but at epizootic population level attacks and easily kills sound trees. In his extensive studies of the severe post war outbreak in Central Europe, SCHWERDTFEGER[12] showed that resinosis is the chief defense of Norway spruce against *I. typographus* and that mass attack by the beetles overcomes this defense. Our data indicate that the mechanism of *I. typographus* effecting such mass attack to overcome the resistance of the host tree is the pheromone attraction produced by the male beetles guided to a suitable host by volatile terpenes[13].

[1] G. B. PITMAN, Science *166*, 905 (1969).
[2] D. L. WOOD, R. H. SILVERSTEIN and M. NAKAJIMA, Science *164*, 203 (1969).
[3] Summarized by J. P. VITÉ and G. B. PITMAN, Proc. XIV Intern. Union Forest Res. Organ., Munich 1967, Section *24*, 683 (1967).
[4] ALF BAKKE, Z. angew. Entomol. *59*, 49 (1967).
[5] E. MERKER, Allg. Forst- u. Jagdztg. *124*, 138 (1953).
[6] C. CHARARAS, *Scolytides des Conifères* (Paul Le Chevalier, Paris 1962), p. 167.
[7] K. G. ADLUNG, Z. angew. Entomol. *45*, 430 (1960).
[8] J. A. RUDINSKY, Contr. Boyce Thompson Inst. Pl. Res. *22*, 23 (1963); Can. Entomol. *98*, 98 (1966).
[9] J. P. VITÉ and R. I. GARA, Contr. Boyce Thompson Inst. Pl. Res. *21*, 251 (1962).
[10] J. A. RUDINSKY, Science *152*, 218 (1966). Terpenes were supplied by K and K Laboratories, Inc., Plainview, New York.
[11] J. A. RUDINSKY, V. NOVÁK and P. ŠVIHRA, Z. angew. Ent., in press.
[12] F. SCHWERDTFEGER, *Pathogenese der Borkenkäfer-Epidemie 1946–50 in Nordwestdeutschland* (Schriftenreihe Forst. Fak. Univ. Göttingen, 1955), vol. 13/14, p. 135.
[13] This study was performed while J.A.R. was at the Institute of Entomology, Prague, on the exchange program of the National Academy of Sciences, and the Czechoslovak Academy of Science and was approved for inclusion in the U.S. International Biological Program.

Sound Production in Scolytidae: Chemostimulus of Sonic Signal by the Douglas-Fir Beetle

J. A. .Rudinsky

R. R. Michael

Abstract. *Stridulation by male* Dendroctonus pseudotsugae *was recorded in response to the natural female attractant (frass) or to three synthetic components of the attractant (frontalin, 3-methyl-2-cyclohexen-1-one, and* trans-verbenol). *This stridulation was acoustically distinct from stress sound and correlated with known attraction behavior. The response of female* D. pseudotsugae *to male stridulation— negation of her attraction—was induced by playback of recorded attractant stridulation but not by that of stress sounds. Acoustic communication must be more important in scolytid behavior than it was heretofore believed to be.*

Although many bark and timber beetles (Scolytidae) stridulate, or produce sound by friction of body surfaces (*1, 2*), there are few behavioral studies of this phenomenon; research has centered on the strong chemical signals of these insects. Stridulatory organs have been recognized in only that sex that does not select the host tree (*1, 2*), and Barr proposed that the function of this sound is to announce the arrival of the stridulating sex to the host-finding, gallery-initiating sex (*1*). With two North American *Ips* species, stridulation is necessary for natural entrance into the gallery of the opposite sex (*1–3*).

In field studies with *Dendroctonus pseudotsugae*, Rudinsky (*4*) found that stridulation by the male beetle at the entrance of the gallery of an attractive female induced the female inside the bark to quickly and entirely negate her chemical attraction for flying beetles. Such an interaction of sonically and chemically induced behavior was not known in any species and was least expected in Coleoptera, since sound production in this order is generally considered to be rudimentary and to have evolved late (5). We have induced this behavior of *D. pseudotsugae* in the laboratory, in the first demonstration with insects of sonic response to chemical stimulus and consequent chemical response.

Since scolytids are known to stridulate in various situations, we looked for distinctive sounds by electronic recording techniques that are used especially with Orthoptera (6). Earlier, Allen *et al.* (7) recorded sounds inside the bark during gallery construction by *D. pseudotsugae*, and Wilkinson *et al.* (3) reported differences in the speed of stridulation during stress and courtship of *Ips calligraphus* (Germar).

Sounds were recorded with a condenser microphone, a low-noise preamplifier, and an instrumentation tape recorder (8). The microphone free-field response was rated flat within 1 db over the frequency range of 20 hz to 25 khz, and tests indicated useful response with negligible resonance to frequencies greater than 40 khz. The preamplifier bandwidth was set with a lower limit of 300 hz to minimize stray acoustic noise and an upper limit of 100 khz. The tape recorder was operated at 152 cm/sec in the frequency modulation mode to achieve maximum bandwidth yet permit time scaling for signal recovery. The recorder bandwidth under these conditions was 0 to 25 khz, and noticeable distortion in the form of ringing occurred for strong signal components with frequencies significantly greater than 25 khz. Although oscillograms indicated major signal energy at frequencies approaching 10 khz with harmonic components well above this range, we believe that the bandwidth limitations of the equipment did not significantly influence the waveform properties that we analyzed.

The amplifier gain setting ranged from 60 to 70 db, depending on the proximity of the specimen, to produce a peak output of about 1 volt. The microphone sensitivity was −60 db referenced to 1 volt/μbar, which indicates a peak sound pressure level of about 1 μbar at about 1 cm from the insect.

Oscillograms were recorded (9) by first establishing a cueing track on the tape to initiate a single oscilloscope sweep just before signal onset. Polaroid photographs of temporally distributed chirps were made at a tape speed of 19 cm/sec.

Beetles tested for both sound production and response came from naturally infested Douglas-fir logs from western Oregon, which were stored at 4°C and brought to beetle emergence temperature as described (10). At least three to five healthy individuals were recorded sequentially in each test situation. Stress stridulation was recorded while the beetle's head and thorax were held by the thumb and forefinger about 1 cm from the microphone. Premating stridulation was recorded both when the male was at the entrance of a female gallery inside the bark of a 50-cm log section (the microphone was 1 cm above the gallery entrance) and when the male was alone but was stimulated by natural and synthetic attractants in the olfactory walkway (10). This walkway, which was used for bioassay during pheromone identification studies (11, 12), was devised to simulate the gallery entrance of an attractive female (10). The walkway was 35 cm long and had a recessed, screened opening for a glass vial of the test compound, over which the male beetle would walk or would stop in the arrestment response (13). This response was known from field observation of male approach to the female gallery.

The arrested males that stridulated were counted without regard to differences in sounds, such as increases in volume or number of chirps before pauses. The number of responses is considered minimal since only naturally audible sounds were included, and control tests with earphones or an oscilloscope showed a general 7 to 8 percent increase in totals. Slow, gentle handling and separate testing of each beetle prevented confusion between stridulation caused by stress and that caused by female attractant, especially since only the latter was accompanied by the typical arrestment behavior. Beetles that fell on their backs and stridulated were not counted or were tested again later.

For statistical analysis of variance in the properties of male stridulation, ten photographs each for stridulation caused by hand pressure, female frass, synthetic attractants, and a live female in a log were selected at random from more than 4000 chirps recorded on tapes. These four kinds of stridulation were then analyzed by number of tooth-strikes per chirp, duration of chirp, and number of tooth strikes per second. Other characteristics were not analyzed; instead, behavior tests were used to determine whether the different sounds functioned as signals.

In the stridulatory organ of male *D. pseudotsugae* (Fig. 1, A and B), two processes on the median posterior margin of the seventh abdominal tergite strike a file of ridges or teeth on the left elytron (*14*). Teeth were counted on the files of 20 beetles; the number of teeth per file was 87 to 137 and the average was 110. When the beetle was held by the head and thorax and observed at ×90 magnification, the stridulatory movement appeared to be slightly upward, back, and downward as the

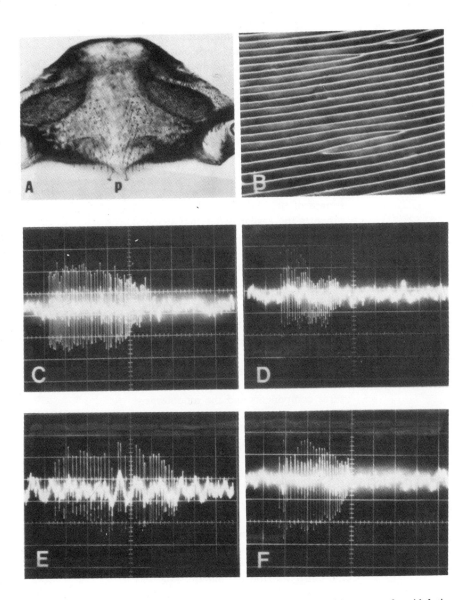

Fig. 1. Stridulatory organ of male *D. pseudotsugae* and oscillograms of stridulation. On the oscillograms (C–F), sound pressure is the ordinate and time (12.5 msec/division) is the abscissa. (A) Micrograph of the seventh abdominal tergite with paired processes (*p*) on the posterior margin which serve as the plectrum (× 62). (B) Scanning electron micrograph of the file of parallel, transverse ridges or teeth on the ventral surface toward the suture and apex of the left elytron. These teeth serve as the pars stridens (× 740). (C) A typical stress chirp of a male beetle held in hand (17 October 1970; 18°C). (D) A typical chirp of a male near attractive female frass (17 October 1970; 18°C). (E) A typical chirp of a male near a live female in attractive frass (13 March 1971; 18°C). (F) A typical chirp of a male near synthetic components of female's attractant (17 October 1970; 18°C).

processes struck the file. Sound occurs only on the downward push, not on the retraction of the abdominal segment, and one movement corresponds to one chirp.

When oscillograms of typical sounds evoked by stress (Fig. 1C) and by the frass of an attractive female (Fig. 1D) are compared, significant differences in the sound properties are seen (*15*).

The distinctiveness of the sound response of the male to female attractant supports the earlier belief that stridulation is a critical part of male attraction behavior (*4*). Therefore we attempted to duplicate the sound with synthetic attractants. Scolytid pheromones often comprise several substances, and in *D. pseudotsugae* there are at least five (*11*). The three identified components are 1,5-dimethyl-6,8-dioxabicyclo[3.2.1]octane (frontalin) (*11*, *16*), 3-methyl-2-cyclohexen-1-one (*11*), and *trans*-verbenol (*12*). We used these three components and the monoterpene camphene, a known host attractant (*17*, *18*), to evoke male stridulation (Fig. 1F). For the properties tested there were no significant differences (that is, differences for which $P > .01$) between stridulation evoked by these substances and that evoked by the natural attractant, female frass. However, when the male was stridulating over a live female in attractive frass (Fig. 1E), significantly more teeth were struck and the chirp was longer, but the rate was the same. This difference may reflect some unidentified chemical not in the frass, tactile stimulus of the log compared to that of the smooth walkway, or a nonchemical interaction between male and female.

Further evidence that this male sound is not an incidental response to the female's attractant is the fact that it occurred with almost 100 percent of

44

the males arrested at attractive frass and up to 88 percent of males arrested at various incomplete combinations of synthetic attractants (Table 1). The difference between totals for arrestment and stridulations might have resulted from the absence of unidentified components or of the tactile stimuli or other stimuli of the entry hole in bark. All established characteristics of the response of bark beetles to attractants are reflected in the stridulation data (at the statistical confidence level of .05), especially the synergism of multicompo-

Table 1. Response of 60 unfed male *D. pseudotsugae* to synthetic attractants in the olfactory walkway. Attractant components are: A, 99.5 percent frontalin; B, 3-methyl-2-cyclohexen-1-one (technical grade); C, 95 percent *trans*-verbenol; fresh Douglas-fir resin; and camphene (technical grade). All substances were diluted to indicated percentages in 95 percent ethanol.

Attractant components	Number of beetles that:	
	Stopped	Stridulated
Complete attractant (♀ frass)	60	59
Resin, A, B, and C	49	37
Camphene, A, B, and C	26	15
Resin, A, and B	43	35
Resin, A, and C	42	26
Resin, B, and C	14	4
Camphene, A, and B	32	21
Camphene, A, and C	45	40
Camphene, B, and C	5	0
A, B, and C	29	16
A and B	28	14
A and C	24	4
B and C	2	1
Resin and A	34	13
Resin and B	30	15
Resin and C	19	5
Camphene and A	30	10
Camphene and B	22	11
Camphene and C	5	0
Resin, 0.01 percent	17	3
Camphene, 0.001 percent	15	1
A, 0.01 percent	17	1
B, 0.001 percent	15	5
C, 0.001 percent	13	1
Ethanol (control)	0	0

nent attractants (*19*) and of host substances. Extensive field tests of these same compounds confirm our results, especially the strong response to frontalin in all combinations, the synergistic effect of *trans*-verbenol and camphene with frontalin, and the low response to most combinations without frontalin (*20*). It had seemed likely that only one component or a single combination of components would evoke sound. However, if male stridulation announces the male presence to the female inside the bark [as Barr suggested (*1*)], there is survival value in variability of the chemical stimulus, since both the female beetle and the host tree show individual variations in the quantities of attractants that they release.

These results demonstrate that the male *D. pseudotsugae* stridulates in response to the chemostimulus of the female attractant, but the male sound cannot be called a signal unless communication occurs. For proof that the female responds, we induced the effect, known from field tests (*4*), in which the stridulation of male beetles over the screened entries of female galleries in the bark caused the female to nullify or mask her attractiveness to flying beetles (*21*).

The female's response to various sounds, live and recorded, was inferred from the behavior of a series of males, each of which either passed by the entrance to her gallery or stopped by it. Each female was tested separately in a log section, and each was checked for attractiveness and the ability to nullify or mask her attraction. In tests in which playback of male sound was used, the males were silenced by excision of their sound organs (*4*) so that they could not evoke or maintain the mask by their own stridulation. A ceramic disk (*22*), 5.1 cm in diameter and 0.6 cm thick, was used as a transducer. The disk was excited, in the thickness expander mode, to a peak voltage of 10 to 15 volts by a power-supply amplifier (23). During playback the disk was mounted in a groove in the bark adjacent to the gallery, its axis perpendicular to the log to allow observation of the male beetles.

The fidelity of sound reproduction at the location of the female in the gallery was not determined. However, the frequency response of the transducer was characterized by the de-emphasis of low frequencies and by resonances throughout the audio spectrum, which varied according to the details of mounting, with the major resonance near 40 khz. The oscilloscope displays and direct auditory monitoring of playback both indicated signal parameters consistent with those used for statistical comparison. Therefore, that the female's response was phonokinesis instead of natural behavior seemed unlikely.

The female's response was induced first by the actual stridulations (not recorded) of normal male beetles nearby, but was not induced by silenced males that were similarly arrested. When the attractant was masked, males showed no repellancy behavior (that is, they did not turn back toward the release point), and they frequently hesitated briefly at the attractant before passing on. No "digging" or klinotaxis occurred. The same behavior was induced by playback of the recorded sounds of a male beetle over the gallery of an attractive female but not by playback of recorded male stress sounds (Fig. 2). Exact time trials were not made, but when stridulation was almost continuous for 2 to 3 minutes the female's lack of attraction became evident a few minutes later (the next males passed without stopping). As was found in field

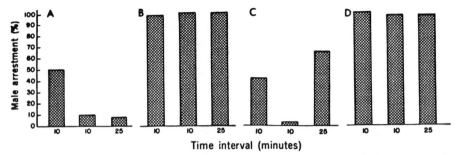

Fig. 2. Response of female *D. pseudotsugae* to male stridulation. This response, in which the female nullifies her attractiveness and that of the surrounding frass, is shown by the failure of male beetles to stop at her gallery entry in a log. The tests were run for 45 minutes; the bars show percentage of tested males that stopped at the gallery entrance in minutes 1 to 10, 11 to 20, and 21 to 45. (A) Normal males were used; their stridulation was the sound stimulus. (B) Silenced males were used; there was no sound stimulus. (C) Silenced males were used; playback of recorded sound made by normal males near a female's gallery was the sound stimulus. (D) Silenced males were used; sound stimulus was playback of stress sounds made by normal males when they were held. These experiments were repeated three times (four with the playback of male sound at the female gallery); each replicate used 40 to 60 fresh males and a new female.

studies (*4*) male sound stimulus appeared to be necessary to maintain the female response as well as to evoke it when the male was kept outside the gallery. After the playback ended, no arrestment occurred for the first 9 to 14 minutes of silence, but then the female apparently stopped the mask. Normal males occasionally stopped and stridulated throughout the tests, presumably because of individual variation in response threshold. Such occasional sound may have served to maintain the female response through the otherwise silent period, since the mask continued longer than it did in experiments with playback and silenced males. Tests were run only 45 minutes, and sound stimulus alone might not suffice to maintain the female response for longer periods.

In nature the male was found to enter the gallery and reach the female fairly soon, and also to stridulate inside the gallery (*7*). Repeated tests confirm the report (*4*) that the female response can occur without stridulation when a silenced male is allowed to contact the female in the gallery.

Two implications of these studies may be clear. (i) Stridulation could be a criterion of olfactory response in bioassay of scolytid attractants and might shed light upon differences between aggregative and sexual aspects of these attractants, which so far are scarcely distinguished. (ii) The soft sounds produced in Scolytidae are short-range signals, and the only long-range signals that are effective in forest terrain must be the chemical ones. However, control and regulation of the attractants—including the duration of their production or release or both, as well as the triggering of masks, inhibitors, or repellants—occur within the aggregated population, where short-range acoustic signals are effective. Busnel (24) has called attention to both (i) the likelihood that a repertoire of low-intensity sound signals will evolve wherever high population density gives them survival value and (ii) the relative importance that acoustic signals have in the hierarchy of animal communication because of their speed, their equidistant transmission in all directions from the source, their impermanence unless repeated, and their relatively great codification.

Like chemical signals they may be "primers" as well as "releasers" and may therefore explain certain physiological puzzles inherent to attempts to explain scolytid aggregation wholly as a series of olfactory mechanisms (25).

The severe environmental damage caused by destructive scolytid beetles dictates that we intensify our study of sonic signals in their aggregation and colonization behavior (26).

49

References and Notes

1. B. A. Barr, *Can. Entomol.* **101**, 636 (1969).
2. J. Schönherr, *Z. Angew. Entomol.* **65**, 309 (1970). The location and form of scolytid phonoreceptors are not known.
3. R. C. Wilkinson, W. T. McClelland, R. M. Murillo, E. O. Ostmark, *Fla. Entomol.* **50**, 185 (1967).
4. J. A. Rudinsky, *Pan Pac. Entomol.* **44**, 248 (1968); *Science* **166**, 884 (1969). There is almost no published data on the interaction of chemically and sonically induced behavior, but the possibilities of animal physiology suggest lack of study rather than the rarity of such interaction. An exception is the work of A. M. Wenner on the honeybee waggle dance, which is summarized in *Animal Communication*, T. A. Sebeok, Ed. (Indiana Univ. Press, Bloomington, 1968), p. 217.
5. B. Dumortier, in *Acoustic Behavior of Animals*, R. G. Busnel, Ed. (Elsevier, New York, 1963), p. 277; R. D. Alexander, T. E. Moore, R. E. Woodruff, *Anim. Behav.* **11**, 111 (1963).
6. See review by R. D. Alexander and references cited therein [*Annu. Rev. Entomol.* **12**, 495 (1967)].
7. D. G. Allen, R. R. Michael, S. A. Stone, *Oreg. For. Lands Res. Cent. Res. Note No. 36* (1958).
8. Hewlett-Packard model 15119A condenser microphone; Princeton Applied Research model 113 low-noise preamplifier; Ampex model FR 1300 instrumentation tape recorder.
9. Tektronix type 565 dual beam oscilloscope.
10. O. K. Jantz and J. A. Rudinsky, *Oreg. State Univ. Tech. Bull. No. 94* (1966).
11. G. W. Kinzer, A. F. Fentiman, Jr., R. L. Foltz, J. A. Rudinsky, *J. Econ. Entomol.* **64**, 970 (1971).
12. J. A. Rudinsky, G. W. Kinzer, A. F. Fentiman, Jr., R. L. Foltz, *ibid.*, in press.
13. "Arrestment" is used in reports on insect behavior to describe the slowing or stopping effect that a chemical substance may have on an insect, as distinguished from attractive or "luring" power. Here the criterion of male arrestment was a full stop over the test vial. In maximum response there were excited attempts to penetrate the screen (this "digging" corresponded to natural male behavior at entering the frass-filled gallery excavated by the female) and the klinotaxis or repeated circling described by D. L. Wood, L. E. Browne, R. M. Silverstein, and J. O. Rodin [*J. Insect Physiol.* **12**, 253 (1966)].
14. A. D. Hopkins, *U.S. Dep. Agr. Bur. Entomol. Tech. Ser. 18, Part I* (1909); S. D. Wood, *Gt. Basin Natur.* **23**, 1 (1963).
15. For all differences $P < .01$ (R. R. Michael and J. A. Rudinsky, in preparation).
16. G. B. Pitman and J. P. Vite, *Ann. Entomol. Soc. Amer.* **63**, 661 (1970); the report that females predominantly respond to frontalin was corrected by M. M. Furniss and R. F. Schmitz, *U.S. Dep. Agr. For. Serv. Res. Pap. INT-96* (1971)
17. J. A. Rudinsky, *Science* **152**, 218 (1966).
18. Frontalin and *trans*-verbenol from Chemical Samples Co., Columbus, Ohio; 3-methyl-2-cyclohexen-1-one from Aldrich Chemical Co., Milwaukee, Wisconsin; camphene from K & K Laboratories, Inc., Plainview, New York.

19. D. L. Wood, R. W. Stark, R. M. Silverstein, J. O. Rodin, *Nature* **215**, 206 (1967).
20. J. A. Rudinsky, M. M. Furniss, L. N. Kline, R F. Schmitz, *Can. Entomol.*, in press.
21. The substance or substances that effect this loss of attractiveness are only now being identified, although an olfactory blocking effect is assumed to be present because the strong residual attractiveness of the frass was also negated without observed repellency behavior (*4*). For convenience the substances responsible are called a "mask." The compound 3-methyl-2-cyclohexen-1-one, which was isolated from hindguts of female *D. pseudotsugae* and arrests walking beetles (*11*) (Table 1), has been shown to prevent flight attraction in extensive field tests in Oregon and Idaho (*20*).
22. Cleavite D8.
23. Hewlett-Packard model 6824A.
24. R. G. Busnel, in *Acoustic Beha'ior of Animals*, R. G. Busnel, Ed. (Elsevier, New York, 1963), p. 69.
25. For example, J. A. A. Renwick and J. P. Vite, *Contrib. Boyce Thompson Inst.* **24**, 283 (1970).
26. We thank L. J. Peterson of the University of California at Davis for the scanning electron micrograph, G. W. Krantz for the micrograph, and M. A. Strand and R. G. Peterson for statistical analysis. Supported by the Oregon State University Research Foundation. This is *Oreg. State Univ. Agr. Exp. Sta. Tech. Pap. No. 3120.*

Multiple Sex Pheromones of the Mealworm Beetle, *Tenebrio molitor* L.

AMONG insects known to use a sex pheromone, it is most common for one sex to respond to the chemical signal produced by the opposite sex[1]. Yet in some species, apparently both sexes respond to the pheromone[2,3], and recently it has been shown, in a few cases at least, that the two sexes may produce distinct pheromones[4,5]. *Tenebrio molitor* has previously been regarded as a classic case: females excite and attract males by means of a sex pheromone[6,7]. There are several pheromones which mediate the reproductive behaviour and physiology of *Tenebrio*, and we have found that the males as well as the females produce sex pheromones. Furthermore, the male pheromones are of two distinct types: (1) an excitant which attracts females and (2) an anti-aphrodisiac which inhibits the response of other males to female scent.

To demonstrate that both sexes produce attractants, groups of ten beetles of the same sex were confined in a small chamber. While unscented air passed through the chamber, the beetles aggregated near the air-outflow. When the airstream was laden with an attractive scent, the beetles rapidly moved to the air-inflow[8]. As Table 1 shows, each sex produces an attractant, and only the opposite sex responds.

When similarly bioassayed, homogenates of either sex yielded analogous results; for example, extracts of males were fifty times more potent towards the females than were extracts of their own sex[9]. But the responses to a mixture of male and female extracts were surprising. When tested on females, the mixture was fully as attractive as its male component, but when tested on males, the mixture was less than one-tenth as potent as the pure female extract. The male component of the mixture somehow seemed to mask the effectiveness of the female component.

Experiments with live beetles showed that males emit an anti-aphrodisiac. One male and one female were used

Table 1. RESPONSE OF MALE AND FEMALE *Tenebrio* TO SCENTS OF LIVE BEETLES

Scent source	Males responding* (per cent)	Females responding* (per cent)
Live male	5	62
Live female	60	9
No scent	6	8

* Each percentage represents pooled results of at least twenty replicates. All beetles were virgin and more than 3 weeks old.

as simultaneous scent sources for the bioassay. The two sexes were inserted into the airstream in three sequences: in parallel to each other; in series with the male upwind from the female; and in series with the female upwind. Each female was tested alone on four chambers of males and then she was tested in combination with the male on four more chambers. (A single female could be used as a source of scent for twenty consecutive tests with no loss of effectiveness.) Only when the female was upwind did the addition of male scent affect the results (Table 2). In such cases, the male in the influent was exposed to female scent; often he was observed to be extruding his genital segments. The male emitted the inhibitory pheromone only after stimulation by female scent. The longer his exposure to female scent, the greater was the inhibitory effect of any given male. In the first, second, third and fourth tests with the female upwind, the male responses (pooled) were 62, 57, 42 and 40 per cent respectively.

A final series of experiments indicated that the male transfers some of his anti-aphrodisiac to the female during mating. Live virgin females were tested for attractiveness in the bioassay, then allowed to mate, and were immediately re-tested. Before mating, 60 per cent of the males responded; after mating, only 47 per cent responded, and this difference is significant by the χ^2 test.

The adaptive significance of the attractant produced by males of *Tenebrio molitor* is obvious: it brings the sexes together for mating. This pheromone may well have additional significance after mating. Females which rushed to the inflow in response to male scent often extruded their ovipositors, suggesting that male scent promotes rapid oviposition. *Tenebrio* females mate many times; as many as six spermatophores may be transferred to a single female in a few hours. Such repeated matings have been reported in other tenebrionids, In one species, *Tribolium castaneum*, Schlager has used a genetic marker (black body colour) to compare the relative utilization of sperm from successive matings. In terms of their tendency to fertilize eggs, sperm transferred in later copulations took precedence over sperm previously sequestered in the spermathaeca[10]. A similar situation probably holds for *Tenebrio*. If so, then the excitant which releases oviposition behaviour and the anti-aphrodisiac play complementary parts; both increase the likelihood

Table 2. RESPONSES OF MALE *Tenebrio* TO THE SCENT OF A LIVE FEMALE AND TO THE COMBINED SCENTS OF A LIVE FEMALE AND A LIVE MALE

Sequence	Female alone* (per cent)	Female + male* (per cent)
In parallel	67 (not significant)	73·5
In series		
Male upwind	70 (not significant)	71
Female upwind	59 ($P < 0.001$, $\chi^2 = 19.0$)	45·2

* Pooled results from at least five replicates.

that a mated female will utilize the freshly transferred sperm before another male chances on her.

This work was supported in part by a grant from the National Communicable Disease Center, US Public Health Service.

[1] Butler, C. G., *Biol. Rev.*, **42**, 42 (1967).
[2] Wood, D. L., and Bushing, R. W., *Canad. Entomol.*, **95**, 1066 (1963).
[3] Eisner, T., and Kafatos, F. C., *Psyche*, Cambridge, **69**, 53 (1962).
[4] Yinon, U., and Schuler, A., *Entomol. Exp. and Appl.*, **10**, 453 (1967).
[5] Alpin, R. T., and Birch, M. C., *Nature*, **217**, 1167 (1968).
[6] Valentine, J. M., *J. Exp. Zool.*, **58**, 161 (1931).
[7] Tschinkel, W., Willson, C., and Bern, H., *J. Exp. Zool.*, **164**, 81 (1967).
[8] Happ, G. M., and Wheeler, J. W., *Ann. Entomol. Soc. Amer.* (in the press).
[9] Berkson, J., *J. Amer. Statistical Assoc.*, **485**, 565 (1963).
[10] Schlager, G., *Ann. Entomol. Soc. Amer.*, **53**, 557 (1960).

Lepidopterous Sex Attractants Discovered by Field Screening Tests[1,2]

W. L. ROELOFS and A. COMEAU

ABSTRACT

New sex attractants were discovered for 37 lepidopterous species in field screening tests with 26 monounsaturated long-chain acetates and alcohols. Interesting taxonomic groupings are discussed in cases where all attracted species of 1 subfamily utilize similar attractant structures. Three situations are discussed in which pairs of closely related species are reproductively isolated in the field by being attracted to different geometrical isomers.

Field screening with various chemicals is an economical way to find new sex attractants. It has been used to find a sex attractant for *Bryotropha similis* Stainton, *Bryotropha* sp. (Roelofs and Comeau 1969), and the pink bollworm, *Pectinophora gossypiella* Saunders (Green et al. 1969, Keller et al. 1969). Field screening studies in which various chemicals are evaporated along with an attractant are also useful in discovering compounds which possess synergistic or inhibitory activity as evidenced by drastic increases or decreases in the number of males trapped (Roelofs and Comeau 1968). Systematic screening tests of both

[1] Approved by the Director of the New York State Agricultural Experiment Station, Geneva, N.Y., as Journal Paper no. 1781, dated Feb. 27, 1970. Received for publication Mar. 6, 1970. This research was supported in part by a Public Health Service Grant no. CCOO287 from the National Communicable Disease Center, Atlanta, Ga. Taken from a dissertation to be submitted by A. Comeau in partial fulfillment of the requirements of the Ph.D. degree at Cornell University.
[2] Cost of expedited printing was paid by Cornell University, New York State Agricultural Experiment Station, Geneva, N.Y.

55

types were made practical by the development of long-lasting polyethylene wicks (Glass et al. 1970), which release chemicals for several months at a low rate, and by the availability of economical fold-up, sticky-coated traps.[3]

This paper reports the results of field screening tests with only single chemicals in efforts to find new sex attractants.

MATERIALS AND METHODS.—Various test chemicals were obtained either from the USDA[4] or synthesized in our laboratories. Ten μliters of each test chemical were injected into a polyethylene cap (Glass et al. 1970) (Scientific Products, OS-6 natural polyethylene closure for 2-dram vial). The caps were placed in 3M traps[3] (Fig. 1) and the traps were hung in various kinds of field environments in sets that included 1 trap for each available chemical.

For live female tests, the females were kept in 3×3-cm screen cages with a vial of water dispensed through a cotton wick. The small screen cage was placed inside the 3M trap. For tests with female extracts, 10 female equivalents (FE) were evaporated on a cotton wick inside the trap.

Moths attracted into the sticky-coated traps were either lifted from the trap or removed by cutting out around them with a razor blade. The moths were cleaned in 3 successive baths of warm chloroform. The chloroform of the last bath was replaced after cleaning 2 moths. The specimens were humidified if needed and pinned for identification.

A chemical is classified as a sex attractant if it attracts only 1 sex of a particular species in several of the sets of traps and if no other chemical or control trap in the sets is attractive to this species. Under these conditions, statistical significance at the 1% level will be obtained from catches of at least 1 moth/set for a given chemical in at least 7 sets of traps. The actual catches often ran into the hundreds. Only male moths were attracted in the present study. A low concentration of each chemical was used in an attempt to simulate natural conditions and take advantage of the tremendous discriminatory ability of the males.

RESULTS AND DISCUSSION.—A sex attractant was discovered for 37 lepidopterous species, including 7 that have not been identified. Only 10 of the 26 chemicals tested were not attractive to moths in this area. The results are summarized in Table 1, which also includes attractants for several species not attracted in our studies but whose pheromone has been identified from female extracts and reported in the literature.

It is obvious from Table 1 that some particular chemicals are attractants for species of several fami-

[3] Central Research Lab, 3M Co., St. Paul, Minn., Patent applied for.
[4] Dr. M. Jacobson and Dr. D. Warthen, Beltsville, Md.

lies, although the males of a given species respond only to one of the compounds. Differing seasonal cycles, diurnal cycles, and habitat preferences can explain reproductive isolation for some species attracted to the same chemical. For example, *Nedra ramosula* Guenée (Noctuidae III) and *Choristoneura fractivittana* Clemens (Tortricidae II) are both attracted to *cis*-11-tetradecenyl alcohol but are active at midnight and 8 PM, respectively. In some cases, particularly in the Noctuidae, the overlap in habitat preference, seasonal cycle, and diurnal cycle is such that these mechanisms alone could not account for reproductive isola-

Fig. 1.—A fold-up sticky coated trap developed by 3 M Co. containing a polyethylene cap wick.

tion. This suggests that secondary chemicals, inhibitors and synergists, may play an important role in reproductive isolation for some lepidopterous species. Secondary chemicals may augment the effect of the attractant chemical and give the females more specificity than obtained with a single chemical.

Some interesting groupings have been found within the subfamilies Olethreutinae and Tortricinae (Tortricidae I and II) but the generalities assumed from these data may have to be modified when the taxonomic sample grows. All of the Olethreutinae species (Tortricidae I) found in our field tests were

57

Table 1.—Lepidopterous species attracted to test chemicals. The family of each species attracted is given along with a reference number to the list of species presented below. Blank areas indicate the compound was not available for testing while an "X" indicates no species attracted.

Position of unsaturation	Carbon length of base compound					
	10	11	12	13	14	16
ACETATES						
cis-5			Gelechiidae: 2,3 Tortricidae I: 11		X	X
trans-5					X	
cis-6						X
trans-6						
cis-7	Gelechiidae: 1		Gelechiidae: 4 Pyralidae: 9 Noctuidae IV: 34,35, 36,37,38,39,40,41,42		Noctuidae I: 22	Gelechiidae: 7 Noctuidae I: 24
trans-7			Tortricidae I: 12		Noctuidae I: 23	
cis-8			Tortricidae I: 13,14			
trans-8			Tortricidae I: 15			

cis-9	- X²			X
trans-9		Gelechiidae: 5 Noctuidae III: 32,33	Gelechiidae: 6 Pyralidae: 10 Noctuidae II: 30	
10 Unidentified species[a]				
cis-11	X^A	Tortricidae II: 16	Tortricidae II: 16,17	Noctuidae II: 25,26,27,28,29
trans-11			Tortricidae II: 18 Phalonidae: 8	
ALCOHOLS cis-9		X		
cis-11	X		Tortricidae II: 19,20,21 Noctuidae III: 31	
trans-11		X		

List of species, with time of flight as observed in 1969

Some chemicals were not available at all times and others were not checked as often as necessary for precise indication of the flight period.

GELECHIIDAE
1 *"Battaristis"* sp. near *nigratomella:* Mid-June; July–August
2 *Scrobipalpa atriplicella* Fischer von Röslerstamm: Mid-May
3 *Chionodes fuscomaculella* Chambers: June 15–30
4 *Filatima* n. sp., *pseudaciella* group: May 27–31
5 *Bryotropha similis* Stainton (a) : July to mid-August
6 *Bryotropha* sp. (a) : July to mid-August
7 *Pectinophora gossypiella* Saunders (b) [b]

PHALONIIDAE
8 *Phalonia* sp.: Late May

PYRALIDAE
9 *Phlyctaenia terrealis* Treitschke: Early June; August
10 *Loxostege neobliteralis* Capps: July 5–15; September

TORTRICIDAE
Subfamily I: OLETHREUTINAE
11 Unidentified: Late May
12 *Argyroploce leucotreta* Meyrick (c) [b]
13 *Grapholitha molesta* Busck (d) : Early June[c]; July–August[c], September
14 *G. prunivora* Walsh (d) : June[c]; July–August[c], September
15 *G. packardii* Zeller (d) : June[c]; July–August[c], September
Subfamily II: TORTRICINAE
16 *Argyrotaenia velutinana* Walker (e) : April–May; July–August; September
17 *Choristoneura rosaceana* Harris: *End of June;* July–August
18 *C. fractivittana* Clemens: 1st week of June
19 *Sparganothis sulfureana* Clemens: June–July[c]; August
20 *S. groteana* Fernald: *Late June;* late July
21 Sp. in Sparganothini: August

60

NOCTUIDAE

Subfamily I: NOCTUINAE
22 *Amathes c-nigrum* L., large sp.: Early July; September–October
23 *A. c-nigrum* L., small sp.: July[c]; September
24 *Euxoa tessellata* Harris: July

Subfamily II: HADENINAE
25 *Orthodes vecors* Guenée, southern sp.: Early June; July–August
26 *O. vecors* Guenée, northern sp.: Early July
27 *O. crenulata* Butler: Early June; July
28 *Scotogramma trifolii* Rottenburg: May; September
29 *Morrisonia confusa* Hübner: May
30 *Polia grandis* Boisduval: Mid-June

Subfamily III: AMPHIPYRINAE
31 *Nedra ramosula* Guenée: Mid-May to early June; August
32 *Spodoptera frugiperda* Abbott and Smith (i) : August[c]; September–October
33 *Apamea interoceanica* Smith: Mid-July

Subfamily IV: PLUSIINAE
34 *Trichoplusia ni* Hübner (f) : Mid-summer[c]; September
35 *Anagrapha falcifera* Kirby: Mid-June[c]; September
36 *Chrysaspidia contexta* Grote: 1st week of June; September[c]
37 *Plusia aereoides* Grote: Early July
38 *Pseudoplusia includens* Walker (h) [b]
39 *Rachiplusia ou* Guenée (h) [b]
40 *Autographa biloba* Stephens (h) [b]
41 *Autographa californica* Speyer (g) [b]
42 *Autographa ampla* Walker: Mid-July

[a] Terminal double-bond: only 1 geometrical configuration possible.
[b] Not attracted in our screening test but reported in the literature.
[c] The test chemical was not present in the field at this time, although other records indicate flight periods at this time.
(a) Roelofs and Comeau 1969.
(b) Green et al. 1969, Keller et al. 1969.
(c) Read et al. 1968.
(d) Roelofs et al. 1969.
(e) Roelofs and Arn 1968.
(f) Berger 1966.
(g) Shorey et al. 1965.
(h) Berger and Canerday 1968.
(i) Sekul and Sparks 1967.

61

attracted to 12-carbon chain acetates. Additionally, the sex pheromone of the false codling moth, *Argyroploce lencotreta* Meyrick (Olethreutinae) has been identified as *trans*-7-dodecenyl acetate (Read et al. 1968). Tortricinae species (Tortricidae II) were attracted by 14-carbon chain acetates or alcohols with the double bond located in the 11-position. The latter compounds are certainly not general among species of this subfamily, since live female or female extracts of 9 Tortricinae species were attractive to their respective males while the test chemicals were inactive. The 9 species in which live females or crude extracts were found attractive to their own males include: *Archips argyrospilus* Walker, *A. mortuanus* Kearfoot, *A. griseus* Robinson, *A. semiferanus* Walker, *Argyrotaenia quadrifasciana* Fernald, *A. juglandana* Fernald, *A. quercifoliana* Fitch, *Sparganothis directana* Walker, and *Pandemis limitata* Robinson. Field tests of the specificity of these females gave results similar to those reported by Roelofs and Feng (1968) except for a number of *A. argyrospilus* males attracted to a *P. limitata* female. Either the attractants involved with these 9 species were not included in the set of chemicals used in our studies or secondary chemicals are required to make them effective.

The use of a common attractant, *cis*-7-dodecenyl acetate, by noctuid species in the subfamily Plusiinae (Noctuidae IV) has been reported (Shorey et al. 1965, Berger 1966, Berger and Canderday 1968). Five of the 9 species listed as attracted by *cis*-7-dodecenyl acetate were observed in our studies. The total catches did not always appear to reflect the high populations of some of the species present in the field, indicating that the single chemical needs to be synergized, or that it is not being released at a competitive rate. The former conclusion is supported by the report of Moorhouse et al. (1969) concerning the noctuid moth *Diparopsis castanea* Hampson. Gas chromatography of the pheromone gland extracts yielded 3 compounds with electroantennogram activity, but only one of them elicits behavioral responses in laboratory bioassays.

Five noctuid species in the subfamily Hadeninae (Noctuidae II) were attracted by *cis*-11-hexadecenyl acetate, including 3 species of *Orthodes*—two of which are sibling species well separated in their seasonal cycle. *Orthodes vecors* (northern species) Guenée is univoltine and flies in early July, while *O. vecors* (southern species) Guenée is divoltine and flies in early June and again in July-August (J. G. Franclemont, personal communication).

A situation was reported recently (Roelofs and Comeau 1969) involving 2 sibling species possessing similar seasonal and diurnal cycles, in which one *Bryotropha similis* Stainton, was attracted to *cis*-9-tetradecenyl acetate and the other was attracted to the geometrical isomer, *trans*-9-tetradecenyl acetate. The wrong isomer for each species was not only unattractive but actually inhibitory to the males. A brief discussion of some of the evolutionary aspects of this situation was given in that report. The present study has uncovered 2 more cases of *"cis-trans* sibling species"*. After identifying the sex pheromone structure of *Grapholitha molesta* Busck (Tortricidae I) from female extracts as *cis*-8-dodecenyl acetate (Roelofs et al. 1969), we found that in the field males of *G. prunivora* Walsh were attracted to the synthetic chemical but not to females of *G. molesta,* indicating the possible role of secondary chemicals. However, males of a 3rd related species, *G. packardii* Zeller were attracted to the *trans* isomer. We now have evidence that males of *G. molesta* are inhibited by the *trans* isomer, similar to the relationships described above for *Bryotropha* spp. Another case of *"cis-trans* sibling species" is found with *cis-* and *trans*-7-tetradecenyl acetate that differently attract specimens of *Amathes* *"c-nigrum"* L. (Fig. 2) which possess subtle differences in size and coloration, and, according to J. G. Franclemont (personal communication), some previously overlooked differences in the genitalia of both sexes. Therefore, these 2 forms are recognized as sibling species reproductively isolated in nature by different sex pheromones. Consequently, the taxonomic status of what was considered a "world-wide species" must be reviewed.

Male moths displayed tremendous discriminatory powers in these studies in consistently being attracted to only 1 chemical out of the 26 presented to them. One case in which a moth was attracted by 2 different chemicals involves *Argyrotaenia velutinana* Walker (Tortricidae II). The sex pheromone was identified as *cis*-11-tetradecenyl acetate (Roelofs and Arn 1968) but this moth is also attracted in the field to *cis*-11-tridecenyl acetate. This situation is currently under further investigation. Apparently when chemicals are released in the field at approximately the "natural" rate of release, male moths are attracted to only 1 specific chemical attractant, as opposed to the less specific responses observed in laboratory bioassays. Possibly further research will show that the sex attractant found in these field screening tests for a particular species is the same as the sex pheromone produced by the female of that species. Studies on several species have been initiated to explore this possibility.

The blank areas in Table 1 show that many potential attractants were not available in this series of long-chain monounsaturated alcohols and acetates. The possibility of finding the sex attractant of an important economic species would be greatly increased if more of these chemicals could be tested and if the whole series was screened in various geographic locations. A complete set of chemicals of the type used for this study would attract only a portion of the lepidopteran species in the area, however, since other

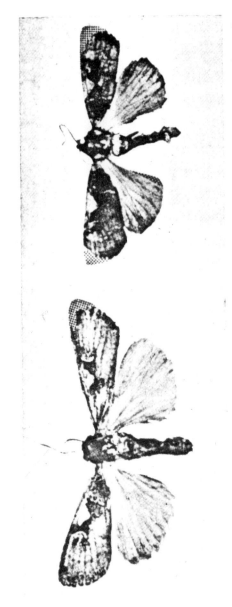

Fig. 2.—Male *Anathes* (Noctuidae I: 22,23) specimens removed from pheromone traps containing *cis*-7-tetradecenyl acetate (large species, left) and *trans*-7-tetradecenyl acetate (small species, right).

types of pheromone structures have been identified (Butenandt et al. 1959, Jones et al. 1966, Roller 1968).

ACKNOWLEDGMENT.—We thank Drs. J. G. Franclemont, R. W. Hodges, E. G. Munroe, P. J. Chapman, S. E. Lienk, and J. F. Gates Clarke for species identifications, and Drs. J. Tette and D. Stearns and Mr. R. Selle for the synthesis of test chemicals, and Drs. M. Jacobson and D. Warthen for generously supplying many test chemicals, and Dr. W. L. Brown, Jr., for reviewing the manuscript.

REFERENCES CITED

Berger, R. S. 1966. Isolation, identification and synthesis of the sex attractant of the cabbage looper, *Trichoplusia ni*. Ann. Entomol. Soc. Amer. 59: 767–71.

Berger, R. S., and T. D. Canerday. 1968. Specificity of the cabbage looper sex attractant. J. Econ. Entomol. 61: 452–4.

Butenandt, A., R. Beckmann, D. Stamm, and E. Hecker. 1959. Uber den Sexual-Lockstoff des Seidenspinners *Bombyx mori*. Reindarstellung und Konstitution. Z. Naturforsch. Teil B 14: 283–4.

Glass, E. H., W. L. Roelofs, H. Arn, and A. Comeau. 1970. Sex pheromone trapping red-banded leaf roller moths and development of a long-lasting polyethylene wick. J. Econ. Entomol. 63: 370–3.

Green, N., M. Jacobson, and J. C. Keller. 1969. Hexalure, an insect sex attractant discovered by empirical screening. Experientia (Basel) 25: 682–3.

Jones, W. A., M. Jacobson, and D. F. Martin. 1966. Sex attractant of the pink bollworm moth: isolation, identification, and synthesis. Science (Washington) 152: 1516–7.

Keller, J. C., L. W. Sheets, N. Green, and M. Jacobson. 1969. *Cis*-7-hexadecen-1-ol acetate (Hexalure), a synthetic sex attractant for pink bollworm males. J. Econ. Entomol. 62: 1520–1.

Moorhouse, J. E., R. Yeadon, P. S. Beevor, and B. F. Nesbitt. 1969. Method for use in studies of insect chemical communication. Nature (London) 223: 1174–5.

Read, J. S., F. L. Warren, and P. H. Hewitt. 1968. Identification of the sex pheromone of the false codling moth (*Argyroploce leucotreta*). Chem. Comm. 792–3.

Roelofs, W. L., and H. Arn. 1968. Sex attractant of the red-banded leaf roller moth. Nature (London) 219: 513.

Roelofs, W. L., and A. Comeau. 1968. Sex pheromone perception. Ibid. 220: 600–1.

1969. Sex pheromone specificity: taxonomic and evolutionary aspects in Lepidoptera. Science (Washington) 165: 398–400.

Roelofs, W. L., A. Comeau, and R. Selle. 1969. Sex pheromone of the oriental fruit moth. Nature (London) 224: 723.

Roelofs, W. L., and K. C. Feng. 1968. Sex pheromone specificity tests in the Tortricidae—an introductory report. Ann. Entomol. Soc. Amer. 61: 312–6.

Roller, H. K., K. Biemann, J. S. Bjerke, D. W. Norgard, and W. S. McShan. 1968. Sex pheromones of pyralid moths—1. Isolation and identification of the sex attractant of *Galleria mellonella* L. (greater wax moth). Acta Entomol. Bohemoslov. 65: 208–11.

Sekul, A. A., and A. N. Sparks. 1967. Sex pheromone of the fall armyworm moth: isolation, identification, and synthesis. J. Econ. Entomol. 60: 1270–2.

Shorey, H. H., L. K. Gaston, and J. S. Roberts. 1965. Sex pheromones of noctuid moths. VI. Absence of behavioral specificity for the female sex pheromones of *Trichoplusia ni* versus *Autographa Californica,* and *Heliothis zea* versus *H. virescens* (Lepidoptera: Noctuidae). Ann. Entomol. Soc. Amer. 58: 600–3.

Gypsy Moth Sex Attractants: A Reinvestigation[1,2,3]

Martin Jacobson, Meyer Schwarz, and Rolland M. Waters

ABSTRACT

Inconsistencies in the attractiveness of synthetic samples of gyptol and gyplure prompted a reinvestigation of their physical, chemical, and biological properties. Although produced by the female gypsy moth, *Porthetria dispar* (L.) pure gyptol, *d*-10-acetoxy-*cis*-7-hexadecen-1-ol, appears to be sexually inert toward the male moth, as does the synthetic homologue, gyplure. The structure previously assigned to the natural sex pheromone must be considered as incorrect.

The detection and possible control of the gypsy moth, *Porthetria dispar* (L.), a serious pest of shade and woodland trees in New England and other eastern States, has involved the collection and rearing of large numbers of virgin females, since the extract of the female abdominal tips, containing the sex pheromone, has been used to bait survey traps. The presence of a gypsy moth infestation was signalled by the appearance of males in the traps. Of necessity, the process was a costly one, and a major effort was therefore devoted to isolating and identifying the sex pheromone. In 1960, *d*-10-acetoxy-*cis*-7-hexadecen-1-ol (gyptol) (I) was proposed as the structure for the sex attractant produced by the female moth (Jacobson et al. 1960). A synthetic sample of the optically inactive form, as well as the resolved *d*- and *l*- forms, were found to be as attractive as the natural isomer (Jacobson 1962). Subsequently, it was

[1] Lepidoptera: Lymantriidae.
[2] Received for publication Apr. 27, 1970. Cost of expedited publication was paid by the authors.
[3] Mention of a proprietary product in this paper does not constitute an endorsement by the USDA.

67

discovered that an 18-carbon homologue, (+)-12-acetoxy-*cis*-octadecen-1-ol (gyplure) (II), was also an extremely potent gypsy moth attractant (Jacobson 1960, Jacobson and Jones 1962).

$$CH_3(CH_2)_5 \overset{c}{C}HCH_2CH{=}CH(CH_2)_2CH_2OH \qquad I$$
$$| \atop OCOCH_3$$

$$CH_3(CH_2)_6 \overset{c}{C}HCH_2CH{=}CH(CH_2)_7CH_2OH \qquad II$$
$$| \atop OCOCH_3$$

This latter finding was considered very important, since gyplure, readily prepared in a 2-step synthesis from commercial ricinoleyl alcohol, offered obvious economic advantages over both the previously used natural extracts and the newly reported natural attractant, gyptol. After extensive field tests of a large sample of laboratory-prepared gyplure, the material was adopted by the U.S. Department of Agriculture in 1962 as the standard lure for gypsy moth survey traps (Jacobson 1965, Statler 1970).

Larger quantities of gyplure were then obtained from commercial sources for the purpose of testing, under field conditions, a new approach to the control of the gypsy moth by the so-called "confusion" method. This proposed method involved the release of large quantities of gyplure in the field with the objective of confusing the flying males, preventing them from locating and fertilizing the nonflying females (Burgess 1964).

However, it was soon discovered that the commercial samples displayed erratic behavior in the field. This behavior could be explained in part by masking of the attractant with large amounts of ricinoleyl alcohol derived from over-saponification of the diacetate (Waters and Jacobson 1965). That this was not the entire explanation became apparent when a large quantity of gyplure, which had been freed of ricinoleyl alcohol by counter-current distribution, as determined by gas-liquid chromatography (GLC) (Jones and Jacobson 1964), rapidly lost all attractancy despite no concomitant changes in GLC patterns. At the same time, preparative thin-layer chromatography (TLC) of active gyplure samples (Collier 1962[4]) revealed that gyplure could be separated from a biologically active component having a much higher R_f value, and that the gyplure itself recovered from the TLC plates was inactive. These results prompted us to reinvestigate the nature of gyplure.

Basic to this investigation was the use of a laboratory bioassay technique, combining the method of Block (1960), which used tethered male moths, with

[4] C. W. Collier, 1962. Plant Protection Division, USDA.

$$CH_3(CH_2)_5CH-CH_2 \xrightarrow[\text{DMSO}]{\text{HC≡CLi·EDA}} CH_3(CH_2)_5\underset{\underset{OH}{|}}{C}HCH_2C≡CH$$

III

$$\xrightarrow[H^+]{DHP} CH_3(CH_2)_5\underset{\underset{OTHP}{|}}{C}HCH_2C≡CH \xrightarrow[\text{2. I(CH_2)_6OTHP}]{\text{1. BuLi (dioxane)}}$$

$$CH_3(CH_2)_5\underset{\underset{OTHP}{|}}{C}HCH_2C≡C(CH_2)_6OTHP \xrightarrow[\text{AcOH}]{\text{AcCl}}$$

$$CH_3(CH_2)_5\underset{\underset{OAc}{|}}{C}HCH_2C≡C(CH_2)_6OAc \xrightarrow{\text{H}_2, \text{ Lindlar}}$$

$$CH_3(CH_2)_5\underset{\underset{OAc}{|}}{C}HCH_2\overset{c}{C}H=CH(CH_2)_6OAc \xrightarrow{OH^-} I$$

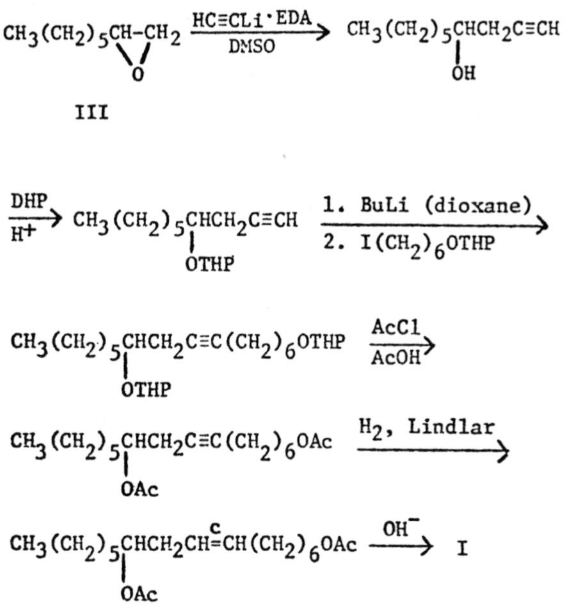

ROUTE B

$$HO(CH_2)_nOH \xrightarrow[\text{2. Ethylvinyl ether}]{\text{1. HCl}} C_2H_5O\underset{\underset{}{|}}{\overset{CH_3}{C}}HO(CH_2)_nCl$$

$$\xrightarrow[\text{DMSO}]{\text{LiC≡CH·EDA}} C_2H_5O\overset{CH_3}{\underset{}{C}}HO(CH_2)_nC≡CH \xrightarrow[\text{2. III}]{\text{1. BuLi}}$$

$$C_2H_5O\overset{CH_3}{\underset{}{C}}HO(CH_2)_nC≡CCH_2\underset{\underset{OLi}{|}}{C}H(CH_2)_5CH_3 \xrightarrow{\text{AcCl}}$$

$$C_2H_5O\overset{CH_3}{\underset{}{C}}HO(CH_2)_nC≡CCH_2\underset{\underset{OAc}{|}}{C}H(CH_2)_5CH_3 \xrightarrow{\text{H}_2, \text{ Lindlar}}$$

$$C_2H_5O\overset{CH_3}{\underset{}{C}}HO(CH_2)_n\overset{c}{C}H=CHCH_2\underset{\underset{OAc}{|}}{C}H(CH_2)_5CH_3 \xrightarrow[\text{CH}_3OH]{\text{AcOH}} I \text{ or } II$$

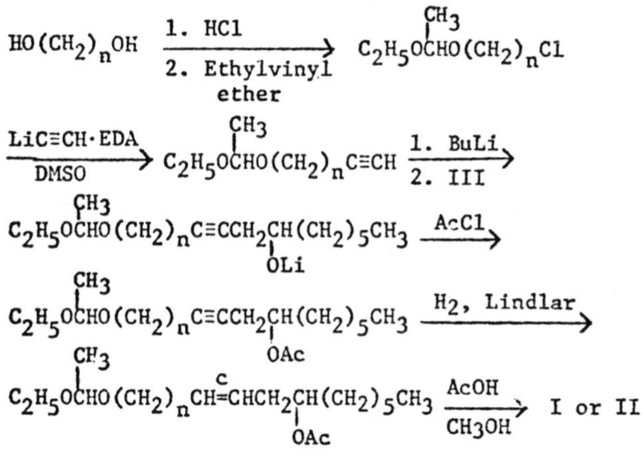

EDA = ethylenediamine, DHP = dihydropyran, THP = tetrahydropyran

Ac = acetyl, DMSO = dimethyl sulfoxide

FIG. 1.—Flow diagram of the reaction sequences used in synthesizing gyptol and gyplure.

the technique of GLC. Thus, a sample of test material was fractionated by GLC and, as the fractions emerged from the chromatograph, they were directed toward the rack of male moths. Emergence of an active fraction was signalled when the males exhibited copulatory motions. With this technique, TLC fractions, column chromatographic fractions, and crude extracts from the abdominal tips of virgin females could all be examined quickly and easily for the presence of active materials. Active fractions from any of the chromatographic techniques could then be trapped and transferred to wicks to be placed in traps for final field testing.

This bioassay technique was first used to corroborate the earlier TLC work of Collier (1962⁴). The results were quite clear-cut, showing that gyplure itself was not attractive to the male moths and that active gyplure samples contained a vanishingly small amount of biologically active material having a much shorter retention time than that of gyplure. These results indicated that either some unknown material in the commercial ricinoleyl alcohol used was attractive per se, or was giving rise to an attractant during the preparation of gyplure. If so, the inactivity of some samples of gyplure as well as the loss of activity demonstrated by other previously active samples could be explained by the absence of such attractants or precursors in some samples of the ricinoleyl alcohol, depending on its origin. Likewise, if the active material or its precursor was present only in very small quantities, degradation or volatilization of the active substance under field conditions could account for the rapid loss of activity.

Gyplure was therefore prepared by total synthesis according to the sequence shown in Fig. 1 (route B). The product was free of ricinoleyl alcohol, but did contain traces of the diacetate. Identity of this completely synthetic gyplure with that of the gyplure prepared from ricinoleyl alcohol was firmly established by GLC, infrared, and nuclear magnetic resonance spectrometry. Field tests[5] and laboratory bioassays proved that this "synthetic" gyplure was inactive as a gypsy moth attractant. The combination of all these data proved conclusively that the previously reported activity of gyplure must have been due to an unknown contaminant in the starting materials used. By the time these data had been established, the stock of survey lure ("active gyplure") was nearly depleted.

The loss of a ready source of survey trap lure threatened the scope of the highly important gypsy moth survey program. To avoid this reduction as well as a return to the use of natural extracts, it was decided to use gyptol in the survey traps as a pri-

[5] Kindly conducted by R. Tardif, Plant Protection Division, Otis Air Force Base, Mass. 02542.

mary standard. Small quantities of gyptol prepared by Jacobson and coworkers in 1960 were still available. The material was field-tested and was consistently found to be as active as the natural extracts even after years of storage.

Additional quantities of gyptol were synthesized according to the procedure shown in Fig. 1 (route B) to assure sufficient supplies for the survey program. Although prepared by a method different from that used earlier (Jacobson et al. 1961), its identity with their gyptol was again established by GLC, infrared, and nuclear magnetic resonance techniques. However, field tests and laboratory bioassays revealed that the material was inactive. Despite the chemical identity of the major components of both samples of gyptol, additional field tests confirmed that only gyptol previously prepared by Jacobson and coworkers in 1960 was active.

To resolve this problem, additional samples of gyptol were then prepared by the earlier method (Jacobson et al. 1961). These newly prepared samples were likewise inactive. In view of this result, the synthesis of gyptol by a 3rd method (Fig. 1, route A) was carried out. Field tests and laboratory bioassays demonstrated the inactivity of this sample. It thus appeared that an erroneous assignment for the active material had been made in our earlier publications, and extracts of the abdominal tips of virgin females were reexamined to resolve 3 points: (1) was gyptol present in the extracts; (2) would the sex pheromone survive the GLC conditions employed; and (3) what retention time would the sex pheromone display?

All 3 points were quickly resolved using the Block-GLC technique. Gyptol was indeed present in relatively large amounts in the extract from virgin female moths. The sex pheromone did survive our GLC conditions. Finally, the sex pheromone had a much shorter retention time than gyptol and was present in exceedingly small quantities.

With these data in hand, the original sample of gyptol prepared by Jacobson et al. in 1960 was examined under the same conditions, using the same laboratory bioassay technique. The results were identical. An active substance eluting far in advance of gyptol was present in Jacobson's synthetic sample. The active substance exhibited the same retention time as that of the attractant in natural extract. Likewise, the retention times of gyptol found in Jacobson's sample, in the natural extract, and in all of our more recently synthesized samples were identical. It thus became apparent that gyptol, although clearly present in the extracts of virgin female gypsy moths, was not the sex pheromone of this insect. Before this work was completed a paper by Eiter et al. (1967) appeared in the literature. These investigators prepared gyptol and gyplure by similar techniques and reported them to be inactive by field and standard Block (1960) bioassays, thus confirming our earlier findings.

Some exploratory work towards establishing the correct structure of the sex attractant of the gypsy moth was then carried out using crude extracts from virgin female moths. Owing to the small quantity of extract available to us, the approach selected was that by which changes in activity of the crude extract could be monitored following chemical transformations. The monitoring technique used was the Block-GLC method. Our preliminary findings established that the attractant was unaffected by basic hydrolysis, ozonolysis, and mild catalytic hydrogenation, but was destroyed by acidic hydrolysis or reduction with lithium aluminum hydride. The activity of the extract appeared to survive pyrolytic conditions (425°C in a 2.54×0.625-cm OD stainless-steel tube packed with crushed Vycor®, N_2 flow rate 20 ml/min) that completely destroyed gyptol and gyplure. It thus appears that the attractant is a substance of relatively low polarity and functionality. It obviously has an extraordinarily high biological activity.

Further work on the resolution of this problem is in progress.

REFERENCES CITED

Block, B. C. 1960. Laboratory method for screening compounds as attractants to gypsy moth males. J. Econ. Entomol. 53: 172–3.

Burgess, E. D. 1964. Gypsy moth control. Science 143: 526.

Eiter, K., E. Truscheit, and M. Boness. 1967. Synthesen von D,L-10-Acetoxy-hexadecen- (7-cis) -ol (1) , 12-Acetoxy-octadecen - (9-cis) - ol - (1) ("Gyplure") und 1-Acetoxy - 10 - propyl - tridecadien - (5-trans. 9) . Justus Liebig's Ann. Chem. 709: 29–45.

Jacobson, M. 1960. Synthesis of a highly potent gypsy moth sex attractant. J. Org. Chem. 25: 2074. 1962. Insect sex attractants. III. The optical resolution of dl-10-acetoxy-cis-7-hexadecen-1-ol. Ibid. 27: 2670. 1965. Insect Sex Attractants, p. 107. Interscience (Wiley) , New York.

Jacobson, M., and W. A. Jones. 1962. Insect sex attractants. II. The synthesis of a highly potent gypsy moth sex attractant and some related compounds. J. Org. Chem. 27: 2523–4.

Jacobson, M., M. Beroza, and W. A. Jones. 1960. Isolation, identification, and synthesis of the sex attractant of gypsy moth. Science 132: 1011–12. 1961. Insect sex attractants. I. The isolation, identification, and synthesis of the sex attractant of the gypsy moth. J. Amer. Chem. Soc. 83: 4819–24.

Jones, W. A., and M. Jacobson. 1964. Insect sex attractants. IV. The determination of gyplure in its mixtures by adsorption and gas chromatography. J. Chromatogr. 14: 22–27.

Statler, M. W. 1970. Effects of gamma radiation on the ability of the adult female gypsy moth to attract males. J. Econ. Entomol. 63 (1) : 163–4.

Waters, R. M., and M. Jacobson. 1965. Attractiveness of gyplure masked by impurities. Ibid. 58: 3:0.

Sex Pheromone Promoting Aggregation and Other Complex Social Behavior

The Gregarisation Pheromone of Locusts

D. J. Nolte, I. R. May and B. M. Thomas

Abstract. Swarming locusts show three physical criteria, i.e. the phase changes of melanisation of the nymphal stages or hoppers, of the proportions of certain body parts (morphometric ratios), and increased genetic recombination (meiotic chiasma frequencies) in the adult. The control of these changes, initiated by aggregation into swarms, i.e. gregarisation, seems to be vested in a pheromone which is produced by all hoppers in both the solitaria and gregaria phases, also by hoppers of the albino strain. Such a pheromone can be extracted from the locust room air and from the locust, these extracts showing high activity in bioassays, primarily in increased chiasma frequencies but also in hopper colour. The extract in risella oil is more efficient than that in petroleum ether and can be distilled to yield an active distillate. The pheromone is secreted in the faeces of hoppers but not of adults. There is evidence in faeces bioassays that all three physical criteria are affected; the pheromone may be called locustone. It is manufactured or secreted in a specific section of the alimentary canal, i.e. the crop. Reception is not through the antennae but through the stigmata. Preliminary chemical analysis of a risella oil air extract distilled into various other solvents showed the presence of a relatively simple saturated aliphatic chain with a carbonyl function, perhaps a ketone or an ester.

Introduction

Gregarisation or swarming of locusts results in phase transformation which is largely density-dependent and is reversible, i.e. the grasshopper or solitaria phase changes into the migrating or gregaria phase, and vice-versa. This transformation is characterised by many morphological, physiological, biochemical and behavioural changes. The morphological effects are mainly in the modification of various ratios in the adult, e.g. the E/F ratio (length of elytron/length of hind femur) increases in gregaria, while the F/C ratio (length of hind femur/width of head) becomes smaller. These ratios have long been one of the main physical criteria of phase transformation (Uvarov, 1921; Faure, 1932). A second criterion is the melanisation of the nymphs or hoppers of locusts in the gregaria phase, large amounts of melanin in the cuticle of the integument being characteristic of all locust species. A third physical criterion has recently been demonstrated to occur in crowded locusts and this is the increase in the frequency of chiasmata formed during meiosis

76

in the adult on crowding, resulting in increased genetic recombination in migrating swarms (Nolte, 1967, 1968).

The study of neurosecretory processes and hormones in locusts is well-advanced, and experimental evidence is available that neurosecretory cells of the pars intercerbralis of the brain produce hormones which activate the corpora cardiaca and corpora allata (Highnam, 1962); the corpora allata have an influence on maturation and sexual behaviour (Pener, 1965); the corpora cardiaca seem to have some effect on melanisation (Staal, 1961). The prothoracic glands differ in size between solitarious and gregarious hoppers (Ellis and Carlisle, 1961); manipulation of the size of these glands in hoppers results in changes in colour like those associated with phase changes, so that hormonal action on phase induction seems also to be indicated for this gland.

Pheromones or external homones have also been demonstrated to play important roles during gregarisation. The first to be discovered was the sex-maturation pheromone of the Desert Locust which advances and synchronises reproduction in swarms (Loher, 1961). Another pheromone was shown to stimulate melanin production in the hoppers of the Desert, African Migratory and Brown Locusts (Nolte, 1963). It was then postulated that for crowded locusts a pheromone accumulates in the atmosphere around a roosting swarm and that this pheromone induces the formation of greater numbers of chiasmata in the chromosomes of the adult as compared with solitaries, specifically in the three long pairs and the five medium-sized pairs (Nolte, 1967, 1968). This pheromone has been extracted from the locust breeding room air in organic solvents such as dimethyl sulphoxide and risella oil and these extracts have been used in bioassays, producing the same effect on solitaries as those changes which occur in a crowded cage of locusts (Nolte, 1968). A fourth pheromonal action has been demonstrated in the stimulation of group-forming behaviour in locusts (Gillett, 1968). It has now been suggested that the last three pheromones are most probably identical and could be called a gregarisation pheromone (Nolte, 1969); this pheromone is assumed to trigger off the process of phase transformation with most of its behavioural, biochemical, physiological, cytological and morphological effects.

The concept of a gregarisation pheromone as the inducer of swarming characteristics in the locust serves as a simple explanation of the mode of action of population density on the locust and warrants further investigation on the reality, the occurrence, the site and mode of production, the chemical properties and the diverse effects of the pheromone. In the present investigation the reality of the pheromone, its extraction in various solvents, its occurrence in the body and excreta and some of its chemical properties were studied.

Materials and Methods

Strains and Cytology. Since change in chiasma frequencies is the most sensitive of the various physical criteria for gregarisation, this test was the most important in the bioassays of this study. The species used was the African Migratory Locust, *Locusta migratoria migratorioides* R. & F., the most important strains being Pretoria-2 and Pretoria-IAB, two substrains of a South African strain originally bred at the Division of Locust Control, Pretoria; Rukwa, a strain derived derived from a collection of solitaries in the Rukwa Valley, Tanzania; Rukwa-S, a substrain of the former and which had segregated an albino mutant; Bothaville, a strain bred from a collection of congregating hoppers in the north-western Orange Free State. Different cagebred generations of these strains were used during the duration of the different experiments of this investigation.

Males were solitarised as follows for most experiments. Third instar hoppers, obtained from crowded cages and thus in the gregaria phase and black in colour, were placed singly in one-litre jars with a continuous supply of green grass. These jars were kept in an isolated room under the same conditions of temperature and humidity as those in the breeding room. Usually these solitaries turn fawn or green at the fourth moult and can be compared with gregarious males from the cages of their origin.

The chiasma frequencies of males from each experiment were scored as totals for the three long chromosomes (3 L) and five medium chromosomes (5 M) from testes stained and squashed in aceto-orcein, counts being made at middiplotene during the first week of adult life; 30 cells were scored for each of 6 males. The 180 cells were treated as a sample extracted from a particular population (experiment) since homogeneity tests show that with a P of generally around 20 % the six individuals of a test were sufficiently alike.

The colours of the various stages of hoppers were noted, special note being taken of loss or retention of melanin as compared with the initial black of the third instar hoppers. Measurements were taken by calipers of the lengths of forewing and hind femur, and of head width.

Extraction of Pheromone. The extraction of pheromone from the air of the locust breeding room was carried out by means of a venturi suction pump through solvents such as petroleum ether and risella oil, for about one month for each extract. Bioassays of the extracts were made on solitarious fourth instar hoppers by moistening a pad of cotton wool with 2.5 ml of the extract and placing this at the bottom of one-litre jar underneath a false floor of wire mesh. The pheromone volatilises from the wad into the air of the jar (Nolte, 1968). Petroleum ether is lethal in the enclosed space but the bioassay of petroleum ether extract was achieved as follows. Most of the solvent was removed in vacuo in a Rotovapor and the remaining liquid was used in the solitary culture jars by applying ten drops to the pad every third day from early fourth instar until each individual had received 2 ml of cencentrated extract. The pure solvent was used in a similar way as control.

To test whether the active pheromone could be removed from the risella oil extract by heating, 750 ml of extract was heated in a boiling flask at 275° C after this had been evacuated, and the material driven off was collected in 5 ml pure solvent which was finally diluted to 50 ml to be used in a bioassay as a concentrated solution.

To investigate the occurrence of pheromone in the body, various body parts of gregarious fourth instar hoppers were extracted in risella oil. In the first extraction 75 abdomens were extracted in 50 ml solvent. In the second the heads, thoraces and abdomens of 75 hoppers were homogenised and centrifuged separately under low temperatures, using 75 ml of solvent for each extract. The yellowish supernatants formed head, thorax and abdomen extracts which were bioassayed on pads in solitary jars as before.

Source of Pheromone and its Receptor. To explore the source of the pheromone further, fresh excreta from the populations of crowded cages was placed below the false bottoms of one-litre jars each containing a solitarious hopper in the fourth instar. These faeces consisted of a mixed lot derived from cages containing hoppers and others containing adults, and the supply to the jars was renewed daily during the fourth and fifth instars; these individuals were compared with control solitaries. In a second experiment the faeces from hoppers only were used, comparing those from gregaria with faeces from solitaria. In the third experiment faeces from crowded hoppers was compared with faeces from crowded adults. In a fourth experiment faeces from hoppers of the albino strain was tested.

Seeing that in the experiment of the previous section the three body parts were complete, i.e. contained the respective parts of the alimentary canal including food and excreta, as well as the haemolymph, an experiment was set up to test extracts of only the relevant parts of the alimentary canal. The foregut consisting of the pharynx, gullet and about two-thirds of the crop of 75 fourth instar crowded hoppers was removed and homogenised in 50 ml risella oil. Similarly the midgut consisting of the gizzard, the ventriculus and caeca but with about the posterior third of the crop was used to make an extract, and the hindgut consisting of the intestine and the rectum with the solid excreta removed from the latter was made into a third extract. In this experiment extracts were also made of the head containing only the brain of 80 fourth instar crowded hoppers, and of the drops of liquid squeezed from the anus of the latter. These five extracts were bioassayed on solitarious fourth instar hoppers. In a final experiment only the crops were removed from 117 crowded fourth instar hoppers, homogenised in 55 ml risella oil and the extract bioassayed in a similar manner.

To test whether perception of the pheromone was through the antennae, the antennae were removed by a cut at the base of the scape in a series of solitarised mid-fourth instar hoppers and these were placed in individual jars with risella oil air extract on a pad underneath a false bottom, and compared with individuals with intact antennae.

Chemical Properties of the Pheromone. An extract of the locust breeding room air (extracted for 1800 hr into 1,700 ml risella oil) was heated to $110°$ C for 1 hr under vacuum in a closed system connected with a container flask of petroleum ether (B.P. 40—$60°$ C). The infrared absorption spectrum of this concentrated solution was run on a Perkin-Elmer Infracord Model 137 spectrophotometer with the following settings: liquid phase, thickness 0.472 mm, interchange E.R., slit program 1,000, gain 3.4, attenuator speed 1,100, scan time 12 mn, suppression off. A similar extract was distilled into 1 ml carbon tetrachloride and the nuclear magnetic resonance spectrum of this was run on a Hitachi Mc 100 with sweep width, 1000 cps. A third extract was distilled into 15 ml benzene and a mass spectrum was run of this solution.

Results

It should be noted that the chiasma frequency figures for controls differ between the various experiments; this is mainly due to genetic differences between the strains as has been shown by Nolte *et al.* (1969). The various results obtained in this investigation may be considered under various headings. In general more importance is attached during bioassays to the chiasma frequencies than to hopper colours or adult morphometrics since during solitarisation the more humid atmosphere in the jars has an overriding effect on loss of melanin and the acquisition of green coloration, while morphometric ratios are affected by the fact that all solitarised individuals start as gregaria under crowded conditions during the first two instars as well as part of the third. Field data for *Locusta* are found in Gunn and Hunter-Jones (1952), the gregaria ratios for males being E/F 2.16, F/C 2.96, and the solitaria ratios being E/F 1.78, F/C 3.67. It should be moted, however, that even in crowded laboratory cages the gregaria figures are never obtained, while the solitaria figures are for individuals which have been solitary during their whole nymphal period. In general the data of bioassays expressed as chiasma frequencies can be taken to show significant differences between any two groups by *c* comparisons where, on the average, a difference of 0.3—0.4 with individual error variances of ± 0.005 indicates a *P* <0.001.

Table 1. *Bioassay of risella oil extract (RO) of locust room air, and of petroleum ether extract (PE). The chiasma frequencies and their error variances are for the three long chromosomes (3 L) and five medium chromosomes (5 M)*

Treatment	Density	3 L		5 M	
		$\bar{x}$	$V_{\bar{x}}$	$\bar{x}$	$V_{\bar{x}}$
A. Stock cage	crowded	6.80	0.00327	6.24	0.00522
Distillate (RO)	1/jar	6.41	0.00637	5.73	0.00728
Control	1/jar	5.91	0.00382	5.20	0.00250
B. PE extract	1/jar	5.51	0.00290	5.30	0.00116
PE control	1/jar	4.69	0.00396	5.13	0.00098
Control	1/jar	4.51	0.00330	5.07	0.00041

Extraction of Pheromone. The results of Table 1 A show the chiasma-inducing effect of the concentrated distillate of an extract of locust room air in risella oil. The treated solitaries had quite high chiasma frequencies and showed a slightly greater retention of black colour than the control solitaries; there were no real differences in morphometric ratios. In Table 1 B it can be seen that petroleum ether extracts the pheromone from the air because the treated males had significantly higher chiasma frequencies, although no differences in morphometric ratios could be found between the three groups; however, the treated individuals all remained dark throughout their instars as compared with the two controls in which the animals lightened considerably in colour.

Presence of Pheromone in the Locust. The results in Table 2 A show that an extract of the abdomens of crowded hoppers in risella oil exerts

Table 2. *Bioassay of extracts of body parts in risella oil: chiasma frequencies*

Body part	Density	3 L		5 M	
		$\bar{x}$	$V_{\bar{x}}$	$\bar{x}$	$V_{\bar{x}}$
A. Abdomen	1/jar	6.83	0.00564	6.00	0.00500
Control	1/jar	5.91	0.00382	5.20	0.00250
Control	crowded	6.80	0.00327	6.24	0.00522
B. Head	1/jar	6.52	0.00665	5.92	0.00393
Thorax	1/jar	6.46	0.00447	5.69	0.00404
Abdomen	1/jar	6.37	0.00568	5.61	0.00498
Control	1/jar	5.62	0.00665	5.42	0.00254
Control	crowded	6.39	0.00428	5.53	0.00453

a strong chiasma-inducing effect on solitaries. This treatment did not effect any retention of gregarious hopper colour nor result in any significant change in morphometric ratios when compared with the control solitaries. The results of Table 2 B show that from all three main body parts a substance can be extracted that raises chiasma frequencies above the level in control solitaries to figures similar to or greater than that of crowded individuals. The morphometric ratios were not significantly affected but retention of gregarious hopper colour during the period of solitarisation was about four times greater for the head extract treatment and about three times greater for the thorax and abdomen extracts than for the control solitaries.

Secretion of Pheromone. In the attempt to determine the method of secretion of the pheromone the results of Table 3 show that in solitaries reared above hopper faeces the chiasma frequencies rose considerably above those in control solitaries, faeces from both solitary and crowded hoppers exerting equivalent effects. Faeces from adults had no effect and the mixed faeces in Table 3 A had a lesser effect than unmixed hopper faeces. Faeces from crowded albino hoppers also had a chiasma-inducing effect. All solitarious hoppers above hopper faeces showed a greater retention of some of the initial third instar black coloration, e. g. in Table 3 C retention was judged to be 65% for the hopper faeces individuals and 25% for both adult faeces and control individuals; in Table 3 D the figures were about 60% and 20% respectively. The shifts in morphometric ratios of individuals exposed to hopper faeces are all in the correct direction and although not large, are especially evident in the F/C ratios.

Source of Pheromone. The results of Table 4 show that, judging by induced chiasma frequency increases, the pheromone is not located in the brain (which does produce hormones), neither in the liquid from the rectum, but that it is located in the alimentary canal, more specifically in the crop. Retention of the initial third instar black coloration

Table 3. *Bioassay of faeces of crowded and solitarised locusts in various instars: chiasma frequencies and morphometric ratios (E/F = elytron length/femur length; F/C = femur length/head width)*

Treatment	Density	Chiasma frequencies				Morphometric ratios	
		3 L		5 M			
		$\bar{x}$	$V_{\bar{x}}$	$\bar{x}$	$V_{\bar{x}}$	E/F	F/C
A. Mixed hopper and adult faeces	1/jar	6.06	0.00359	5.58	0.00213	1.85	3.42
Control	1/jar	5.37	0.00303	5.32	0.00139	1.81	3.54
B. Crowded hopper faeces	1/jar	6.65	0.00562	6.01	0.00365	1.94	3.19
Solitary hopper faeces	1/jar	6.69	0.00425	6.03	0.00365	1.95	3.16
Control	1/jar	5.64	0.00398	5.45	0.00221	1.92	3.25
C. Crowded hopper faeces	1/jar	6.75	0.00416	6.07	0.00558	1.92	3.26
crowded adult faeces	1/jar	5.45	0.00465	5.32	0.00125	1.94	3.43
Control	1/jar	5.56	0.00457	5.55	0.00186	1.92	3.39
Control	crowded	6.43	0.00385	5.91	0.00290	1.97	3.18
D. Crowded albino hopper faeces	1/jar	6.61	0.00422	5.92	0.00285	1.89	3.35
Control	1/jar	5.30	0.00440	5.29	0.00166	1.88	3.38
Control	crowded	7.03	0.00335	6.33	0.00379	1.92	3.34

Table 4. *Bioassay of extracts of various body parts in risella oil: chiasma frequencies and morphometric ratios*

Body part	Density	Chiasma frequencies				Morphometric ratios	
		3 L		5 M			
		$\bar{x}$	$V_{\bar{x}}$	$\bar{x}$	$V_{\bar{x}}$	E/F	F/C
A. Foregut	1/jar	6.77	0.00428	5.96	0.00289	1.83	3.43
Midgut	1/jar	6.51	0.00376	5.72	0.00235	1.90	3.37
Hindgut	1/jar	5.15	0.00507	5.23	0.00147	1.89	3.32
Head with brain	1/jar	5.16	0.00424	5.25	0.00151	1.86	3.35
Anal drops	1/jar	5.29	0.00427	5.28	0.00147	1.85	3.35
Control	1/jar	5.20	0.00454	5.24	0.00142	1.87	3.38
Control	crowded	7.11	0.00211	6.29	0.00351	1.94	3.29
B. Crop	1/jar	6.66	0.00372	6.05	0.00318	1.94	3.32
Control	1/jar	5.30	0.00440	5.29	0.00166	1.88	3.38
Control	crowded	7.03	0.00335	6.33	0.00379	1.92	3.34

Table 5. *Bioassay of antennal removal: chiasma frequencies and morphometric ratios*

Treatment	Density	Chiasma frequencies				Morpho- metric ratios	
		3 L		5 M			
		$\bar{x}$	$V_{\bar{x}}$	$\bar{x}$	$V_{\bar{x}}$	E/F	F/C
Antennaless							
RO extract	1/jar	6.30	0.00540	5.47	0.00363	1.92	3.41
Control	1/jar	5.61	0.00362	5.23	0.00265	1.83	3.56
Control	crowded	6.22	0.00368	5.74	0.00278	1.87	3.21

was greater for individuals treated with crop and foregut extracts than for individuals with midgut or hindgut extracts or with extracts of head with brain or of anal drops or of control solitaries; for these categories, in that order, retention percentages were judged to be 65, 65, 30, 20, 16, 16, 16. The shifts in morphometric ratios of treated individuals in Table 4 A were rather heterogeneous, but the changes in the ratios in the croptreated individuals in Table 4 B, although not large, were in the correct direction.

In a search for the receptor of the pheromone the data of Table 5 show no depressing effect of loss of antennae on the chiasma-inducing effect of risella oil air extract; these individuals also retained more of the initial black than did the control solitaries, and their morphometric ratios were nearer those of crowded populations than were those of the controls.

Chemical Properties of the Pheromone. Although risella oil is suitable as solvent of the pheromone for bioassays it is not suitable for chemical analyses. The first chemical tests applied proved to be unsatisfactory because the solutions of the pheromone in the three solvents petroleum ether, carbon tetrachloride and benzene appear to have been much too dilute. The infrared absorption spectrum of the petroleum ether solution appeared to indicate the presence of a relatively simple substance with two sharp peaks at 1,722 and 1,212 cm^{-1} respectively, absorptions which are diagnostic for carbonyl stretching. The absence of bands beyond 3,000 cm^{-1} indicated the exclusion of alkene, alkyne and aromatic groups and thus the presence of only a straight chain aliphatic compound with a carbonyl function.

The nuclear magnetic resonance spectrum also appeared to indicate the presence in the carbon tetrachloride of a simple substance with a basic structure of $R{-}O{-}CH_2 \cdot CH_3$. The mass spectrum data were the most unsatisfactory with no concrete substance appearing but only what appeared to be impurities such as ether.

Discussion

The investigation on the extraction of the pheromone from the atmosphere of the locust breeding room confirms data of previous investigations (Nolte, 1968). Risella oil is a good solvent and being inert the pheromone can be expelled from solution in it. It has now been shown that whereas petroleum ether extracts have previously been found to be lethal in bioassays, the concentration of the extract and the application of it in small amounts leave a residue which is active in inducing increased chiasma formation and in the retention of some of the initial black coloration in solitarised hoppers. These extracts, however, had no effect on the adult morphometric ratios which constitute a third criterion of phase transformation in locusts. Possibly, for such changes, a constant stimulation supplied in small amounts is necessary.

It was at first thought that the abdomen would prove to be the source of the pheromone, and thus two separate experiments for the extraction of abdomens in risella oil were set up. The stronger chiasma-inducing effect of the more concentrated extract (Table 2 A) demonstrates the quantitative effect of the pheromone. If this effect is additive it appears that head extracts in risella oil contain more of the pheromone than do extracts from equivalent numbers of thoraces or abdomens. Since the main organs left in situ in the three separated body parts were the nervous system and the alimentary canal, it appeared at this stage that secretion of the pheromone was in either of these organs.

In the experiments on extracts of body parts no positive effect could be detected on morphometric ratios but in the bioassay in Table 2 B the treated solitarised hoppers did retain more of the black gregarious coloration than did the control solitaries.

The bioassay with hopper faeces showed a positive effect in increasing chiasma frequencies, in greater retention of black hopper coloration and in slightly less solitaria-like morphometric ratios than in controls, in fact the faeces acted as if it carried a gregarisation pheromone. Two important facts emerging from these experiments are that both gregaria and solitaria produce this pheromone and that such production occurs only in the hopper stages and not in the adult. If the pheromone is secreted in the faeces it must be in liquid form in the gut and could perform its function efficiently only for a congregated mass of hoppers where an accumulation of the pheromone would result in raising it above the threshold value; with solitaries this value would not be reached.

A re-evaluation of the bioassay with extracts of the three body parts would now indicate that the extracted pheromone could have been present in the haemolymph, the partly digested food and the faeces of these parts. In the results of Table 4 A it became evident that the head containing the brain only had no pheromone neither was this present in the liquid expressed from the anus nor in the hindgut minus its faeces. The pheromonal effect was, however, expressed by the fore- and midgut extracts, the former containing the greater part of the crop, the latter only the posterior part. The crop extract confirmed these results in that it showed the location of the pheromone in this section of the alimentary canal: this extract modified all three physical criteria of gregarisation towards those of the gregaria phase and the active ingredient could be called *locustone*.

Although Loher (1961) thought that perception of the maturation pheromone, synchronising reproduction in the Desert Locust, could mainly be through the antennae, the present investigation on the removal of antennae does not support the hypothesis of antennal perception of the gregarisation pheromone. Most probably perception is through the stigmata directly into the haemolymph.

Knowledge of pheromones has advanced to the point where certain generalisations may be made in respect of their chemistry (Wilson, 1963). The pheromone bombykol of the silkworm moth has the constitution $C_{16}H_{29}O$, and generally these sex attractants have relatively high molecular weights (180—300) which accounts for their narrow specificity and high potency. The molecular weights of the alarm substances of ants are lower but they do not exhibit the stimulation potency of the sex attractants; for example, the constitution of citral is $C_9H_{15}O$. These alarm substances often have little specificity. One of the bark beetle attractants which has been analysed, shows the molecular composition of $C_8H_{14}O_2$ and a molecular weight of 142 (Kinzer *et al.*, 1969); this pheromone is released in the faeces. These pheromones of *Dendroctonus* spp. are population-aggregating and are not species or sex specific (Pitman *et al.*, 1969). Among the few pheromones of which the structural formulae are known a variety of chemical substances occur: among the sex attractants that of the silkworm moth is a doubly unsaturated alcohol with conjugated double bonds, that of the gypsy moth is an acetate of an unsaturated alcohol, and that of the honeybee queen is an unsaturated acid with a methyl ketone group; of the ant alarm substances citral is an unsaturated aldehyde with removed double bonds, and citronellal is an unsaturated aldehyde with a double bond; the bark beetle attractant is a cyclic octane. The chemical work on locust-one will have to be extended, with the collaboration of a team of chemists: at the moment it seems to be a relatively simpler substance than the above-mentioned pheromones. It may, however, be of a similar nature as these pheromones in that it is an aliphatic chain, with a ketone function. Acetone, ethyl acetate and methyl acetate have been found emanating from crowded mature Desert Locusts; these substances have been shown to be excreted through the anus but are not responsible for the maturation-accelerating effect in this locust (Blight *et al.*, 1969). In our work only the nymphal stages produce locustone but it has been postulated (Nolte, 1968) that in the adult a modified form of the pheromone may be produced. Locustone may thus be related to acetone and the acetates.

Acknowledgement. We are greatly indebted to Dr. B. Staskun of the Department of Chemistry including Biochemistry for the use of the infrared spectrophotometer and for advice on the analysis of the spectrum, and to Dr. K. Pachler and Dr. S. Eggers of the C.S.I.R., Pretoria, for running the nuclear magnetic resonance and mass spectra respectively.

References

Blight, M. M., Grove, J. F., McCormick, A.: Volatile neutral compounds emanating from laboratory-reared colonies of the desert locust, *Schistocerca gregaria.* J. insect Physiol. **15**, 11—24 (1969).

Ellis, P. E., Carlisle, D. B.: The prothoracic gland and colour change in locusts. Nature (Lond.) **190**, 368—369 (1961).

Faure, J. C.: The phases of locusts in South Africa. Bull. ent. Res. **23**, 293—424 (1932).

Gillett, S.: Airborne factor affecting grouping behaviour in locusts. Nature (Lond.) **218**, 782—783 (1968).

Gunn, D. L., Hunter-Jones, P.: Laboratory experiments on phase differences in locusts. Anti-Locust Bull. (Lond.) No 12, 35 p. 1952.

Highnam, K. C.: Neurosecretory control of ovarian development in *Schistocerca gregaria.* Quart. J. micr. Sci. **102**, 57—72 (1962).

Kinzer, G. W., Fentiman, A. F., Page, T. F., Foltz, R. L.: Bark beetle attractants: identification, synthesis and field bioassay of a new compound isolated from *Dendroctonus.* Nature (Lond.) **221**, 477—478 (1969).

Loher, W.: Die Beschleunigung der Reife durch ein Pheromon des Männchens der Wüstenheuschrecke und die Funktion der Corpora allata. Naturwissenschaften **48**, 657—661 (1961).

Nolte, D. J.: A pheromone for melanization of locusts. Nature (Lond.) **200**, 660—661 (1963).

— Phase transformation and chiasma formation in locusts. Chromosoma (Berl.) **21**, 123—139 (1967).

— The chiasma-inducing pheromone of locusts. Chromosoma (Berl.) **23**, 346—358 (1968).

— Chiasma-induction and tyrosine metabolism in locusts. Chromosoma (Berl.) **26**, 287—297 (1969).

— Dési, I., Meyers, B.: Genetic and environmental factors affecting chiasma formation in locusts. Chromosoma (Berl.) **27**, 145—155 (1969).

Pener, M. P.: On the influence of corpora allata on maturation and sexual behaviour of *Schistocerca gregaria.* J. Zool. **147**, 119—136 (1965).

Pitman, G. B., Vite, J. P., Kinzer, G. W., Fentiman, A. F.: Specifity of population-aggregating pheromones in *Dendroctonus.* J. Insect Physiol. **15**, 363—366 (1969).

Staal, G. B.: Studies on the physiology of phase induction in *Locusta migratoria migratorioides* R. et F. Publ. Fds. Landb. Exp. Bur. No 40, 1—125 (1961).

Uvarov, B. P.: A revision of the genus *Locusta* L. (= *Pachytylus* Fieb.) with a new theory as to periodicity and migration of locusts. Bull. ent. Res. **12**, 135—163 (1921).

Wilson, E. O.: Pheromones. Scientif. Amer. **208**, 100—110 (1963).

A LOCUST PHEROMONE: LOCUSTOL

D. J. NOLTE, S. H. EGGERS, and I. R. MAY

Abstract—For some time a gregarization pheromone has been postulated, and demonstrated, to account for the changes which take place in solitary locusts when they are crowded, i.e. for phase transformation. The airborne substance which is given off by locust faeces has been extracted and submitted to ultra-violet, infrared, mass, and nuclear magnetic resonance spectroscopy. The results indicated a derivative of guaiacol, which is a degradation product of the metabolism of the lignin of plants. This airborne substance is 2-methoxy-5-ethylphenol and has been synthesized and bioassayed on solitary phase locust hoppers. It proved positive in action on the quantitative phase traits such as increased chiasma frequencies during meiosis, melanization of hopper integument, changed adult morphometric ratios, and the behaviour of hoppers: this pheromone has been named locustol.

INTRODUCTION

AFTER it had long been known that phase transformation of locusts is a phenomenon resulting from swarming, it was discovered that an airborne factor or pheromone is given off so that in the crowded conditions in the breeding room of our Locust Unit the process of melanization appears to be stimulated in the hoppers of the desert, the tropical migratory, and the brown locust (NOLTE, 1963). During this same period an outbreak of the brown locust occurred in the Karoo plateau of South Africa, and it was discovered that during meiosis in the swarming male the frequency of chiasmata (the occurrence of genetic crossing-over) increased by as much as 30 per cent over that of solitary males (NOLTE, 1967). Investigations on laboratory-reared populations of all three species then demonstrated that the rise in frequency is the result of crowding and gregarization, so that in addition to colour change of the hopper and modified morphometric ratios of the adult, a third quantitative criterion could be added, i.e. on crowding there is an increase in the frequency of chiasmata in the eight longest of the eleven autosomes.

Various bioassays and tests were conducted on the air of the locust breeding room and it was demonstrated, through the use of air extracts in water, risella oil 17, and dimethylsulphoxide, that a pheromone is produced which activates the increase in chiasma frequency, therefore a chiasma-inducing pheromone (NOLTE, 1968). At this time it was shown by GILLETT (1968) that a pheromone stimulates group-forming behaviour in locusts, and it was then suggested that the three pheromonal actions could be the result of a single pheromone, being produced by hoppers, and termed the gregarization pheromone. Further bioanalyses conducted on solitary hoppers (NOLTE et al., 1970) showed that the chiasma-inducing pheromone is excreted in faeces by solitary and gregarious hoppers, but not by adults. Pheromonal production has been traced to the crop section of the alimentary tract, and sensory perception appears to be through the spiracles directly into the haemolymph. Bioassays carried out with air extracts and faeces showed that these were positive in their effects on melanization, i.e. the retention of melanin in solitarising gregarious third instar hoppers. The effect of this pheromone on adult morphometric ratios, if any, is not clear although some correlation has been found to exist between increased chiasma frequencies in treated solitary and shifts toward gregariform ratios (NOLTE et al., 1970).

The theory then is that during gregarization the atmosphere around roosting swarms of hoppers becomes concentrated with the pheromone which then causes a reactive haemolymph in the hoppers.

Initial work on the petroleum ether extracts of the locust breeding room air indicated that these were too dilute for chemical analysis (NOLTE and MAY, unpublished). The forerunner of the attempt to chemically characterize and synthesize the pheromone was to bioassay the effects of various chemical substances on phase characteristics, such substances being used as contaminants in the atmosphere of jars containing solitary hoppers (NOLTE and MAY, unpublished). Substances which were analogous to the action of the pheromone, i.e. increased chiasma frequencies considerably, were ethyl formate, acetone, and dihydroxy-acetone; methyl formate did not increase these frequencies but retained full black colour in solitary hoppers.

The present research was initiated as a co-operative attempt to extend such tests, to identify the chemical structure of the pheromone, and, if possible, to synthesize it.

MATERIALS AND METHODS

Bioassays of extracts and solutions were made using as test animals various strains of Locusta migratoria migratorioides which were taken from crowded stock cages as hoppers in their third instar and thus gregarious, i.e. black in colour. Each hopper was placed in a 1 l. solitary jar and provided with a constant supply of fresh green grass. The test extract or solution was added to the jar in 1 ml aliquots: 1% aqueous solutions were dropped on a wad of cotton wool on the bottom of the jar, generally twice per instar. Pentane solutions had to be applied dropwise because high solvent concentrations in the air proved toxic to the hoppers. These test animals were compared with their controls for colour change during the various instars, for chiasma frequencies during the first few days after becoming adults, and for adult morphometric ratios. Chiasma frequencies, being the most sensitive index of gregarization, were taken as the main criterion in our evaluation of the test material which served as guide-posts in the investigation.

To score for chiasmata, 30 cells from each testis of young adult males were studied in 6 to 8 experimental animals and the same number for the controls. The testes were squashed, stained in aceto-orcein, and in order to minimize the variability which may occur between the follicles (SHAW, 1971), the testis was rubbed on blotting paper, removing the fat, and then spread on two or three slides so that when squashed the contents of the follicles were mixed: this yields a more random sample for the scoring of chiasmata. Only the eight longest autosomes were scored since the three shortest almost invariably have one chiasma per pair. The significance of differences was calculated by analysis of variance. Analyses of variance have shown that for *Locusta* the between-cells-within-males component of variance is very similar under the conditions of the various experiments, and that the percentage difference in chiasma frequency between treatment and control gives a fair indication of the statistical significance of differences. Thus generally a difference of at least 6 to 7 per cent between the two groups can be accepted as significant at the 0·02 per cent level of probability.

A change of colour was noted as follows. Since each solitarisation was commenced with third instar hoppers from crowded cages and therefore gregarious in colour, solitarisation started with loss of colour (melanin). Any bioassay that affects this loss thus has to be judged on the amount of retention of black during the period of treatment of the hopper: this is a somewhat subjective method but is workable.

The morphometric ratios of adults were obtained by measuring the length of the elytron (E), the length of the hind femur (F), and the greatest width of the head (C) by means of calipers.

A large number of substances were bioassayed for activity during chiasma-formation. Preliminary work was on aqueous extracts of locust breeding room air. Such extracts were treated with (1) sodium metabisulphite to eliminate ketones, (2) boric acid to complex alcohols, and (3) sodium bicarbonate to neutralize acidic compounds. Loss of activity would indicate that the pheromone would belong to that particular class of compounds.

Since the active principle is excreted in faeces the most promising method of preparative-scale isolation was the steam distillation of faeces (1 kg), followed by pentane extraction of the distillate. Steam distillate was passed through cationic (IR 120) and anionic (IRA 400) ion-exchange resins. For further purification the pentane extract of the steam distillate was exhaustively extracted with 1 N sodium hydroxide; this in turn was saturated with gaseous carbon dioxide and re-extracted with pentane. After such treatment the pentane extract was thoroughly dried over magnesium sulphate, filtered, and the solvent removed *in vacuo* at reduced temperature so as to minimize losses. A brownish oil with a distinctive smell was obtained (27 mg). This was subjected to preparative thin-layer chromatography on Merck silica gel plates, 2 mm thick, with methylene chloride as solvent. Two major, as well as traces of several minor, compounds were visible when viewed under u.v. light.

Gas chromatography of the pentane extract (Packard, 5% OV-101 on chromosorb, 90° for 5 min, programmed to 150° at 10°/min, nitrogen flow rate 30 ml/min f.i.d. detector) showed two major and several minor components.

The techniques of bioassaying the effects of various substances on the behaviour of locust hoppers are still being surveyed: the main difficulty lies in controlling the diffusion rates of volatile substances. Initial attempts consisted of using a square box and lid, painted black inside and provided with an observation slide and a light suspended from the middle of the lid. On the floor a piece of white paper was placed, with squares in four rows of four each. The substance to be tested was placed as a drop or two between squares 2 and 3 of the first row, 1 per cent solutions in distilled water being used; for the controls a drop of water was used. A fourth instar hopper was then placed on the centre of the paper and its position on the squares noted after 5, 10, and 15 min.

OBSERVATIONS

The data in Table 1 show the mean chiasma frequencies, with their standard errors, of the eight longest autosomes (also expressed as percentages) of the test animals treated with aqueous extracts of room air, to which the various inactivating agents had been added. It is quite evident that aqueous extracts contain no active

TABLE 1—THE MEAN CHIASMA FREQUENCIES, WITH STANDARD ERRORS, OF THE EIGHT LONGEST AUTOSOMES OF INDIVIDUALS TESTED WITH AN AQUEOUS EXTRACT OF LOCUST ROOM AIR AND SUCH AN EXTRACT WITH ADDITIVES

| Substance tested | Mean chiasma frequency | | Significance |
	No.	As %	
Aqueous extract	$12\cdot88 \pm 0\cdot174$	100	
Aqueous extract + sodium metabisulphite	$13\cdot17 \pm 0\cdot134$	103	
Aqueous extract + sodium bicarbonate	$11\cdot25 \pm 0\cdot255$	88	$P < 0\cdot001$
Aqueous extract + boric acid	$13\cdot21 \pm 0\cdot174$	103	

ketones or alcohols, but an active substance that is acidic. Table 2 provides further evidence for this: the steam distillate of faeces contains an active principle which continues to remain active in a pentane extract, and furthermore is acidic since an anionic resin removes the acidic principle.

The main components of the gas chromatography of the pentane extract had retention times of 6 and 11 min, respectively. Zones A and B on the thin-layer plate, corresponding to the two major components, were eluted with methylene chloride to yield 5 mg and 10 mg, respectively.

TABLE 2—THE MEAN CHIASMA FREQUENCIES, WITH STANDARD ERRORS, OF THE EIGHT LONGEST AUTOSOMES OF INDIVIDUALS TESTES WITH STEAM DISTILLATE OF FAECES AND VARIOUS EXTRACTS OF THIS

| Substance tested | Mean chiasma frequency | | Significance |
	No.	As %	
Control	$10\cdot82 \pm 0\cdot157$	100 ⎫	$P < 0\cdot01$
Steam distillate	$12\cdot95 \pm 0\cdot155$	119 ⎬	
Pentane extract of above	$12\cdot13 \pm 0\cdot112$	112 ⎭	
Distillate adsorbed on IR 120	$12\cdot42 \pm 0\cdot218$	115 ⎫	$P\ 0\cdot01$
Distillate adsorbed on IRA 400	$10\cdot95 \pm 0\cdot158$	101 ⎬	

Zone A: a small amount was deposited on spectrographic graphite and examined mass spectroscopically (AEI MS9, direct insertion). A molecular weight of 124 was observed. The accurate mass found was 124·051; $C_7H_8O_2$ requires 124·052. Nuclear magnetic resonance (Varian HA100, $CDCl_3$ TMS as internal standard) showed the presence of methoxyl (τ 6·2, three protons, singlet), four aromatic protons (multiplet) while the remaining proton was unresolved. It was suspected that the substance was guaiacol or an isomer thereof. Gas chromatographic comparison (conditions as above) of the three isomers confirmed that the substance was guaiacol. The three isomers were bioassayed (Table 3); the o- and p-isomers showed the greatest activity.

TABLE 3—THE MEAN CHIASMA FREQUENCIES, WITH STANDARD ERRORS, OF THE EIGHT LONGEST AUTOSOMES OF INDIVIDUALS TESTED WITH THE THREE ISOMERS OF GUAIACOL

Substance tested	Mean chiasma frequency		Significance
	No.	As %	
p-Methoxyphenol	13·04 ± 0·079	119	$P < 0.001$
o-Methoxyphenol	12·99 ± 0·089	118	$P < 0.001$
m-Methoxyphenol	12·01 ± 0·093	109	P 0·01
Control	10·96 ± 0·095	100	

Zone B: mass spectroscopy (conditions as for zone A) showed a molecular weight of 152. The accurate mass found was 152·084; $C_9H_{12}O_2$ requires 152·084. Nuclear magnetic resonance (same conditions as for zone A) showed the presence of an aromatic methoxyl (τ 6·2, three protons, singlet), an aromatic ethyl group (quartet at τ 7·42, two protons; triplet at τ 8·8, three protons), three aromatic protons (multiplet), the final proton once again being unresolved. This compound was thus suspected as being an ethylmethoxyphenol of which several isomers are possible.

Based on the assumption that the pheromone could be an enzymatic degradation product of lignin, 2-methoxy-4-ethylphenol and 2-methoxy-5-ethylphenol were considered likely possibilities (Fig. 1). Both isomers were synthesized

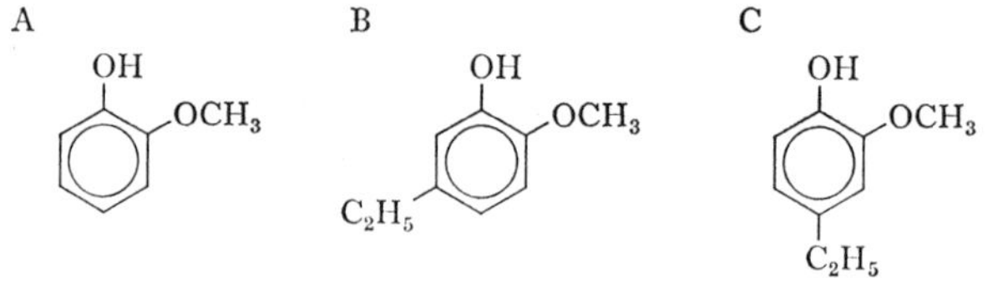

FIG. 1. A, guaiacol. B, 2-methoxy-5-ethylphenol. C, 2-methoxy-4-ethylphenol.

(COULTHARD et al., 1930; GOLDBERG and TURNER, 1946). Of these the 5-ethyl isomer proved to be identical with the isolated substance (by gas chromatography and mass spectrometry). Both isomers were bioassayed (Table 4) and both showed considerable activity in chiasma increase, with that of the 5-ethyl isomer the greater.

During the course of this investigation various chemical substances were bioassayed, as side-issues, and a few that may be named, with their activities in chiasma production, are *p*-hydroxyphenyl acetone (113%), phenyl acetyl carbinol (111%), and vanilla (114%), the latter being related to guaiacol.

TABLE 4—THE MEAN CHIASMA FREQUENCIES, WITH STANDARD ERRORS, OF THE EIGHT LONGEST AUTOSOMES OF INDIVIDUALS TESTED WITH THE TWO ISOMERS OF METHOXY-ETHYLPHENOL

| Substance tested | Mean chiasma frequency | | Significance |
	No.	As %	
2-Methoxy-5-ethylphenol	$13 \cdot 43 \pm 0 \cdot 100$	127	$P < 0 \cdot 001$
2-Methoxy-4-ethylphenol	$12 \cdot 72 \pm 0 \cdot 149$	121	$P < 0 \cdot 01$
Crowded cage	$11 \cdot 75 \pm 0 \cdot 125$	112	$P < 0 \cdot 02$
Control solitaries	$10 \cdot 53 \pm 0 \cdot 093$	100	

In the present investigation not much importance was attached to the colour change of hoppers, because one disadvantage of rearing hoppers in 1 l. jars is that the atmosphere inside the jars easily attains a high humidity: such humidities facilitate greening of hoppers, and greening in *Locusta* seems to reduce melanin deposition.

Retention of black is judged subjectively, and on this basis the test animals of Table 2 show a 20 per cent retention by the control and IRA 400 treatment, a 40 per cent retention by the distillate and IR 120 treatment, and a 60 per cent retention by the pentane extract. The test animals of Table 3 show a 10 per cent retention by the control and the m-isomer of guaiacol, while the o- and p-isomers show a slightly higher retention at 20 per cent; a strange phenomenon in this experiment was the appearance of several coffee-coloured individuals in each of the guaiacol tests. The test animals of the experiment in Table 4 showed a 25 per cent retention of black by the control, 40 per cent by the 4-ethyl isomer, and 80 per cent by the 5-ethyl isomer.

Since raised chiasma frequencies are the most sensitive index for gregarization not much importance was attached to morphometric ratios in the preliminary work, but the data for the experiments in Tables 3 and 4 are given in Table 5. It should be noted that none of the treatments with any of the isomers of guaiacol produced any significant deviations from the control, but that the two isomers of ethylphenol both produced significantly lower F/C ratios. It should also be noted that for the guaiacols these ratios showed greater differences than did the E/F ratios.

The preliminary results for the behavioural tests are given in Table 6. A hopper may stay quiet during the period of the test, move randomly from square to square, move away from the area where the spot is, move towards it, or start marching round and round the cage (this is a characteristic of groups of gregarious hoppers in such boxes). It is evident that guaiacol (o-methoxyphenol) exerts no influence on hopper movement, but that both isomers of methoxy-ethylphenol are activators of gregarious behaviour or act as attractants.

Substance tested	E/F	F/C
p-Methoxyphenol	$1{\cdot}91 \pm 0{\cdot}015$	$3{\cdot}41 \pm 0{\cdot}041$
o-Methoxyphenol	$1{\cdot}90 \pm 0{\cdot}018$	$3{\cdot}47 \pm 0{\cdot}038$
m-Methoxyphenol	$1{\cdot}91 \pm 0{\cdot}028$	$3{\cdot}54 \pm 0{\cdot}036$
Control	$1{\cdot}90 \pm 0{\cdot}018$	$3{\cdot}45 \pm 0{\cdot}028$
None of these values differ significantly from the control		
2-Methoxy-5-ethylphenol	$1{\cdot}98 \pm 0{\cdot}045$	$3{\cdot}19 \pm 0{\cdot}029$*
2-Methoxy-4-ethylphenol	$1{\cdot}94 \pm 0{\cdot}020$	$3{\cdot}11 \pm 0{\cdot}051$†
Crowded cage	$1{\cdot}93 \pm 0{\cdot}057$	$3{\cdot}33 \pm 0{\cdot}063$
Control solitaries	$1{\cdot}99 \pm 0{\cdot}046$	$3{\cdot}35 \pm 0{\cdot}057$

* Significant at $P\ 0{\cdot}05$.
† Significant at $P < 0{\cdot}05$.

TABLE 6—THE RELATIVE BEHAVIOUR OF HOPPERS EXPOSED TO AN ATMOSPHERE WITH DIFFUSING GUAIACOL AND THE TWO ISOMERS OF ETHYLPHENOL. THE NUMBER OF HOPPERS WITH EACH TYPE OF BEHAVIOUR IS EXPRESSED AS A PERCENTAGE

Test substance	Marching	Near spot	Far from spot	Random	Stationary
o-Methoxyphenol	—	14	21	15	50
Control	—	14	29	14	43
2-Methoxy-4-ethylphenol	11	39	14	11	25
Control	—	7	28	15	50
2-Methoxy-5-ethylphenol	13	31	13	9	34
Control	—	13	14	9	64

DISCUSSION

It appears from the chemical analysis and bioassays presented that 2-methoxy-5-ethylphenol possesses all the properties exhibited by the substance extracted from hopper faeces. This pheromone has been called locustol and can be synthesized from guaiacol (o-methoxyphenol) which is a degradation product of lignin. It is postulated that the lignin ingested in grass or shrubs is degraded in the crops of larvae to guaiacol, some of which is excreted in faeces and the rest changed to locustol and also excreted.

The data collected in this investigation do not unequivocally demonstrate that the three quantitative criteria of gregarization are interrelated through the action of the pheromone. The rise in chiasma frequencies is undoubtedly the result of a pheromone because the increases are high, are quantitative, and serve as a fine criterion of crowding on the application of the pheromonal extract. Pigmentation of hoppers is too much under the influence of external factors such as the humidity

94

of the atmosphere. High humidity, which occurs often in the jars used for bio-assays, causes greening, and various investigations in our Unit have demonstrated that an increase of green pigment (a mixture of carotenoid and mesobilirubin) seems to depress the production level of melanin. Notwithstanding this depression, locustol has been shown to significantly decrease the loss of melanin in solitarising hoppers.

The case of morphometric ratios of adults is under even more severe restrictions. In the first instance it is generally found that cage-bred populations never attain the morphometric ratios exhibited by extreme phases, for which E/F is higher for gregaria while the F/C is lower. Secondly, since the method of bioassaying is to use hoppers of the third instar, reared in crowded stock cages, these are already on their way to developing gregariform ratios. DIRSH (1953) has shown that for the desert locust the F/C ratio is the more valuable since this ratio does not overlap in the extreme phases: in this investigation the two isomers of the methoxy-ethylphenol do show some effect on this ratio in solitarising animals.

The preliminary tests on the behaviour of hoppers also show that these two isomers encourage gregarious movement when compared with guaiacol. Using these facts, with the necessary qualifications, as a base for judging the measure of gregarization, locustol or 2-methoxy-5-ethylphenol comes closest to satisfying the requirements of a general gregarization pheromone. Although this isomer can be regarded as the true pheromone, it is evident that there are several other compounds each possessing varying degrees of activity, affecting one or other of the gregarization traits.

Acknowledgements—We wish to express our thanks to Dr. B. STASKUN of the Department of Chemistry for the initial spectroscopic tests of the locust room air extract. We are also deeply indebted to LORÉ PILLMAN of the Zoology Department for carrying out the tests on the behaviour of hoppers, and to Miss K. WEISS of N.C.R.L. for technical services.

REFERENCES

COULTHARD C. E., MARSHALL J., and PYMAN F. L. (1930) The variation of phenol coefficients in homologous series of phenols. *J. chem. Soc.* **1930**, 280–291.

DIRSH V. M. (1953) Biometrical studies on phases of the desert locust. *Anti-Locust Bull. Lond.* **16**, 1–34.

GILLETT S. (1968) Airborne factor affecting grouping behaviour in locusts. *Nature, Lond.* **218**, 782–783.

GOLDBERG A. A. and TURNER H. S. (1946) The chloracetylation of guaiacol. *J. chem. Soc.* **1946**, 111–113.

NOLTE D. J. (1963) A pheromone for melanization of locusts. *Nature, Lond.* **200**, 660–661.

NOLTE D. J. (1967) Phase transformation and chiasma formation in locusts. *Chromosoma, Berl.* **21**, 123–139.

NOLTE D. J. (1968) The chiasma-inducing pheromone of locusts. *Chromosoma, Berl.* **23**, 346–358.

NOLTE D. J., MAY I. R., and THOMAS B. M. (1970) The gregarisation pheromone of locusts. *Chromosoma, Berl.* **29**, 462–473.

SHAW D. D. (1971) Genetic and environmental components of chiasma control—I. Spatial and temporal variation in *Schistocerca* and *Stethophygma*. *Chromosoma, Berl.* **34**, 284–301.

Chemical Defense of Brood by a Social Wasp

ROBERT L. JEANNE

Abstract. *Ants are a constant threat to the nests of tropical social wasps. Adults of the neotropical social wasp* Mischocyttarus drewseni *apply a secretion to the nest stem which is repellent to ants foraging for food by scouting and recruiting, and effectively keeps them from gaining access to the nest and discovering the brood.*

Because of their ubiquity in tropical habitats and the readiness with which so many of their species attack social wasps, ants are a constant threat to the nests of these insects. They are generally believed to have had a major influence on the evolution of the life cycle and social organization of the wasps (*1*). It is almost mandatory for even the shortest-lived colonies to have some means of defending their brood, although this aspect of wasp biology has received little attention. I have discovered the defense strategy evolved by the primitively social wasp *Mischocyttarus drewseni* (*2*). The following observations and experiments were made in the field near Santarém, Pará, Brazil.

The nest of *M. drewseni* consists of a simple paper comb suspended by a narrow vertical stem 2 to 3 cm long. To discover the brood of such a nest, a scout ant must first descend this narrow stem. The initial hypothesis was that the chance of an ant's discovering this stem was so small that most colonies completed their cycle (about 6 months) before they happened to be discovered. Two sets of observations suggest that this is not the case. First, brood removed from the nest and placed directly on the substrate (leaves, twigs, under eaves of houses, and so forth), or on the ends of pins stuck into the substrate (to simulate the nest stem) were always discovered by ants within a matter of

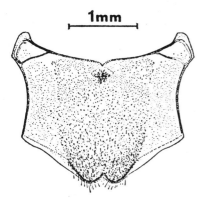

Fig. 1. Terminal gastral sternite of *Mischocyttarus drewseni*. At the anterior margin is the small nonsclerotized area bearing the tuft of hair. Reproduced from van der Vecht (*4*).

Fig. 2. A female *Mischocyttarus drewseni* applying the ant repellent secretion by rubbing the tuft of hair on the terminal sternite against the surface of the nest stem.

hours, evidence of the rapidity with which ants will discover food. Second, even when this was done next to an active wasp nest, so that ants by the hundreds were milling about the base of the nest stem, the nest remained undiscovered. An alternative hypothesis was that the adult wasps (usually less than 30 per colony) actively defend the brood by removing ants from the nest stem as they attempt to descend. In one experiment one wasp larva was placed on each of four insect pins, which were then stuck into the substrate around the stem of an active nest, each pin 5 cm from the stem. Then all the adult wasps were removed from the nest. Within an hour all four of the larvae on the pins were covered with ants [*Monomorium pharaonis* (*3*)]. Far from ignoring the nest itself, ants constantly explored the base of the stem and many descended partway (96 in 11 minutes); none succeeded in getting more than one-third of the way down before turning around and going back up. Two hours later the nest was still untouched, yet ants were still attempting to descend the stem. This indicated that the adults do not actively defend the nest, rather that the nest stem itself is in some way repugnant to ants, and that the effect lasts for several hours at least.

To determine whether this effect was due to some physical characteristic of the material of the nest stem itself, or to some material on it that has to be renewed by the adult wasps, ants (*Monomorium pharaonis*) were given the choice of traversing the stem of an active nest or one from a nest that had been abandoned for several months. In 36 trials only two ants chose the active stem. This suggested that the adult wasps kept the stem in an "active" condition.

At the base of the terminal gastral

97

sternite of female *Mischocyttarus* is a small nonsclerotized area bearing a tuft of long hairs (*4*) (Fig. 1). This tuft often appears moist in living wasps. At frequent intervals, individuals rub this tuft against the surface of the nest stem and upper parts of the nest. In a typical sequence a worker moves to the top of the nest rubbing the tip of the gaster over the nest surface, then approaches the nest stem headfirst, turns her body and reaches as high as she can (about 17 mm) up the stem with the gaster and rubs the stem for 1 or 2 seconds before rubbing down to the top of the nest again, where rubbing ceases (Fig. 2). This is done an average of 0.6 times per hour on a typical nest (*5*). I suggest that the tuft carries a secretion which is brushed onto the stem, where it is effective in repelling ants.

The following experiment was devised to test this hypothesis. Glass capillary tubes 65 mm long were fastened vertically in a row by placing them over the points of pins pushed up through a cardboard platform. A small cube of Brazil nut meat was forced onto the top of each tube as ant bait. Two series of experiments were run. In both series half the tubes were provided with a smear of secretion (10 to 15 mm long) by rubbing them against the tuft of hair of from one to four living wasps. In the first series the control tubes were left unsmeared, whereas in the second series, they were smeared with a variety of available substances chosen to simulate the physical properties of the wasp secretion (Table 1). Experimental tubes were alternated with control tubes on the test platform. The test platform was then placed in a room where *Monomorium pharaonis* foragers were common. Within a short time scout ants would discover the tubes and begin to explore them. The following data were recorded for each tube: (i) the number

Table 1. Relative effectiveness of the secretion from the terminal gastral sternite (experimental tube) in keeping ants from baits placed on the tops of glass tubes. Each tube was watched until ten ants succeeded in reaching the bait. The number of ants failing to reach the bait during this period is given. When less than ten ants reached the bait, the number succeeding was recorded and is shown in parentheses. The superscript letters refer to the materials used to smear the control tubes in experiments 8 through 12, as follows: a, fifth (penultimate) sternite of two *M. drewseni*; b, fourth sternite of two *M. drewseni*; c, water; d, terminal sternite of an unidentified eumenine wasp; e, salivary fluid of *M. drewseni*; f, Vaseline.

Experiment No.	Ants failing to reach bait (No.)	
	Experimental tube	Control tube
Control tube not smeared		
1	24	2
1	44	7
1	63	3
2	51	2
2	5	5
3	5 (0)	4
3	2 (0)	0 (1)
3	17	1
4	10	12
4	37	3
4	22 (8)	6
5	2	3
5	3	1
5	72	2
6	11	0
6	166 (2)	0
6	16	0
7	25	0
7	8	0 (1)
Control smeared with control substances		
8	47	2[a]
8	20	0[a]
8	94	1[a]
9	8	4[b]
9	239	2[b]
9	26	2[b]
10	96	2[c]
10	110	4[d]
10	67	1[e]
11	39	1[e]
11	2	0[e]
11	30(0)	13(0)[f]
12	358(0)	3[e]
12	202	0[e]
12	74	2[e]

of ants to ascend the tube partway, turn around, and descend; and (ii) the number of ants to reach the bait at the top of the tube. When ten ants had reached the bait on a given tube the number of ants to ascend only partway was totaled (Table 1). The number of ants turning back before reaching the bait is significantly greater for the tubes smeared with secretion from the terminal gastral sternite of *M. drewseni* than for the control tubes, as determined by the Mann-Whitney U test ($P < .001$).

It is clear that the secretion is an effective ant repellent. Whether its effectiveness is due to its chemical or to its physical nature is not so clear. However, when ants contacted a smear of secretion with their antennae they often retracted violently from it, then groomed their antennae extensively, an indication that the smear was repugnant to them. This repugnance seemed to be sensed entirely by the antennae; the ants never brought their mouthparts into contact with the material, and there was no evidence that they found it sticky to the touch. On the other hand, the control materials never elicited behavior suggesting that they were repugnant. The smear of Vaseline, somewhat thicker than the others, apparently presented a physical barrier (6).

Such a barrier at the access to the nest effectively eliminates the need for adult wasps to be present on the nest at all times to guard against ants. This is especially important in the tropics for species such as *Mischocyttarus* in which a single female may found a colony. The period prior to the emergence of the first adult offspring is the most critical for such colonies, for the founding female must leave the nest unattended while foraging. Defense of the type evolved by *M. drewseni* en-

ables her to do so without increasing the risk that the nest will be discovered by ants during her absence.

The nest stem of *M. drewseni* is admirably adapted to chemical means of defense. An important requirement is that ants be presented with as long a chemical barrier as possible. The long stem (2 to 3 cm) of the nest and the elongated first abdominal segment of the wasps (Fig. 2), enabling them to apply secretion over most of this long stem, have apparently evolved together toward this end. All members of the group *M. labiatus*, to which *M. drewseni* belongs, have elongated first abdominal segments, and all construct nests with elongated stems. The small diameter (0.5 to 1.0 mm) of the stem, as well as its smooth, nonabsorbent surface, are features which minimize the amount of secretion required to keep the stem adequately covered. Thus, the characteristics of this defense mechanism suggest that an evolutionary balance between effectiveness and economy has been achieved.

The repellent properties of the secretion are probably ineffective against army ants (*Eciton* spp.), which forage en masse and are not easily thwarted. The mass foraging technique is eminently adapted to overcoming colonies of social insects (7); my observations indicate that there is nothing that the adult wasps can do in the face of a raid by army ants but abandon the nest and sacrifice the brood. But the chance that a nest will fall in the path of such a raid is apparently low enough for most colonies to mature and produce sexuals before being attacked. The scouting and recruitment technique is much less spectacular than mass foraging, but my impression is that ants which use this method are much more efficient at finding food, and are much more likely to be first on the scene when food becomes available. The fact that *M. drewseni* has evolved an effective defense against ants of this type, but not against army ants, suggests that it is the former group that presents the most serious threat to the survival of these wasps.

Van der Vecht (*4*) found that members of the genera *Polistes, Para-* *polybia,* and *Ropalidia* (except the subgenus *Icarielia*) also possess a tuft of long hair at the base of the last sternite. Each of these genera constructs uncovered, stemmed nests consisting of a single comb. These facts suggest that chemical defense of the *Mischocyttarus* type might occur in other genera in the Vespidae.

References and Notes

1. O. W. Richards and M. J. Richards, *Trans. Roy. Entomol. Soc. London* **102**, 1 (1951).
2. *Mischocyttarus* (Hymenoptera, Vespidae) is a New World genus ranging from southwestern Canada to northern Argentina, with the greatest species diversity in the Amazon basin; *M. drewseni* ranges from northern South America to southern Brazil. The observations cited in this paper were made in the Lower Amazon region of Brazil.
3. *Monomorium pharaonis* is a small (2 mm in length) trail-laying species which uses the scouting and recruiting method of foraging. These ants will readily attack wasp brood.
4. J. van der Vecht, *Kon. Ned. Akad. Wetensch. Proc. Ser. C Biol. Med. Sci.* **71**, 411 (1968).
5. Based on 520 hours of observation on 20 colonies.
6. Samples of the secretion have been sent to Dr. James Gaylor at Cornell University for analysis.
7. E. O. Wilson, *Evolution* **12**, 24 (1958).
8. I thank Senhoras Erica and Violeta Hagmann of Santarém, Pará, Brazil, for hospitality shown me while the field work was conducted; and Dr. T. Schoener for advice on statistics; Dr. E. O. Wilson, Dr. W. L. Brown, Dr. B. Hölldobler, D. Woodruff, Nancy Lind, and Kathleen Horton for criticism of the manuscript. Supported by NSF predoctoral fellowships and by grants from the Evolutionary Biology Fund of Harvard University.

CITRAL IN STINGLESS BEES: ISOLATION AND FUNCTIONS IN TRAIL-LAYING AND ROBBING

M. S. BLUM, R. M. CREWE, W. E. KERR, L. H. KEITH,
A. W. GARRISON, and M. M. WALKER

Abstract—The mandibular gland secretion of workers of the stingless bee *Trigona subterranea* is dominated by geranial and neral, the two stereoisomers of citral. This terpene is a powerful attractant for workers of *T. subterranea* and is the primary trail-following compound utilized by this species. Workers are either repelled or they exhibit attack and alarm behaviour in the presence of very high concentrations of citral.

Citral is also produced by the robbing bee *Lestrimelitta limao*. Workers of *Melipona* and *Trigona* species, which are normally robbed by *L. limao*, appear to be completely disoriented by high concentrations of citral. The behaviour of species of bees which are not attacked by *L. limao* is not drastically altered in the presence of this terpene aldehyde. Citral is identified as the probable key factor responsible for the successful robbing activities of *L. limao* workers. The rôle of exocrine products which are employed as allomones by robbing bees and ants is discussed.

INTRODUCTION

IN MANY species of stingless bees, worker recruitment is accomplished by means of highly efficient trails which are laid by scout bees (LINDAUER and KERR, 1958). These 'aerial' trails originate from a series of droplets of mandibular gland secretion which are deposited at rather specific intervals between the food find and the nest. Relatively volatile compounds present in the mandibular gland secretions ensure that 'aerial' trails, which are capable of recruiting substantial numbers of bees in a short period of time, can be rapidly generated. In terms of the time taken to recruit large numbers of workers, the scent trails utilized by some species of *Trigona* are considerably more efficient than the dances of the honey bee (LINDAUER and KERR, 1958). In addition, these scent trails can transmit information in the vertical component whereas the honey bee dances cannot.

In order to be able to analyse in depth the trail-laying behaviour of stingless bees, it seemed highly desirable to identify the chemical stimuli employed, and the present investigation describes the chemistry and biological functions of the mandibular gland products of *Trigona subterranea* Friese. This species belongs to the subgenus *Geotrigona*, which contains species which often nest in the ground and are characteristically rather shy. On the other hand, species in this subgenus have a highly efficient system for recruiting workers to food sources which are at considerable distances from the nest. Significantly, when workers of *T. subterranea* are collecting either pollen or nectar, they are strongly odoriferous whereas bees which are not actively foraging are not characterized by easily detectable odorants (LINDAUER and KERR, 1960). The obvious fragrance of a collecting worker of *T. subterranea* reflects the presence of freshly secreted mandibular gland constituents which are being utilized to generate a chemical trail as a necessary prelude to recruiting. We have established that the principal pheromone utilized by *T. subterranea* is the oxygenated terpene, citral, a compound isolated previously from *Lestrimelitta limao* (Fr. Smith) (BLUM, 1966), a stingless bee which is an obligatory robber. We have also studied the rôle that citral plays in the biology of *T. subterranea*. In addition, we have examined the responses of several species of bees to this compound in order to attempt to gain some insight into the part that this terpene may play in the robbing biology of *L. limao*.

MATERIALS AND METHODS

Gas chromatography

Initially, the glandular source of the volatile constituents was determined by analysing extracts of salivary, hypopharyngeal, and mandibular glands. Extracts were prepared in 1,1,2-trichlorotrifluoroethane (Freon 113), dried over anhydrous sodium sulphate, and concentrated under vacuum to a small volume. Subsequently, the analyses were made on extracts of whole heads derived from free-flying workers. Workers were collected in Ribeirão Prêto, S.P., Brazil.

The volatiles present in the extracts of *T. subterranea* were analysed on a Micro-Tek 220 gas chromatograph employing 6 ft $\times$ 0·25 in. o.d. glass columns containing 15% FFAP on Chromosorb W, 60/80 mesh. After injection the column was maintained at 100°C for 5 min and then temperature programmed up to 180°C at a rate of 5°C/min. Isothermal analyses were made on a column of 10% Carbowax 20M on Aeropak 30, 100/120 mesh, at 164°C. The carrier gas (nitrogen) had a flow rate of 60 ml/min. Quantitative estimation of the volatile compounds was determined by simultaneous recording from a Disc integrator.

Mass spectroscopy

A Perkin–Elmer 900 gas chromatograph was interfaced to a Hitachi RMU-7 mass spectrometer, and the column effluent was split to afford continuous monitoring by both the flame ionization detector and the ion current monitor of the mass spectrometer. The gas chromatographic column was a 50 ft support, coated, open tubular unit coated with 5% Carbowax 20M on Anakrom ABS. Instrumental conditions were as follows: gas chromatographic column temperature 110°C, interface temperature 150°C, mass spectrometer ion source temperature 210°C, and electron energy 70 eV.

102

Thin-layer chromatography

The concentrated extract was spotted on Eastman silica gel plates and developed with 2% ethyl acetate in *n*-hexane. Spots were rendered visible by spraying with saturated 2,4-dinitrophenylhydrazine in 2 N HCl.

Biological investigations

The responses of workers of *T. subterranea* to citral were determined by employing foraging bees which originated from mature colonies.

The reactions of different species of bees to citral were determined by placing a small wooden block (6 mm × 2 mm) impregnated with the neat terpene either near the entrance or just inside the entrance of observation hives. The responses to citral of the following species were examined: *Trigona (Paratrigona) subnuda* Moure, *T. (Plebeia) droryana* Friese, *T. (Nannotrigona) testaceicornis* (Lep.), *T. (Frieseomelitta) varia* (Lep.), *T. (Scaptotrigona) postica* Latr., *Melipona rufiventris* Lep., *Apis mellifera adansonii* Latr., and *Bombus atratus* Frank. With the exception of *A. mellifera*, which synthesizes citral in the Nassanoff gland, none of these species are known to produce this terpene.

RESULTS

Thin-layer chromatography

Solvent development revealed the presence of a single reddish-orange spot which was made visible with 2,4-dinitrophenylhydrazine. This carbonyl-containing constituent had an R_f value of 0·70 and was converted to a brown colour after subsequent spraying with KOH. The behaviour of citral was identical in all respects after thin-layer chromatographic analysis.

Gas chromatography

Two components accounted for more than 95 per cent of the volatiles detected when the extracts were chromatographed on both the FFAP and the Carbowax columns. On FFAP these compounds had retention times of 17 and 18 min and on Carbowax 3·9 and 4·5 min. Neral and geranial, the two stereoisomers of citral, had identical retention times when analysed on the two stationary phases. Neral, the *cis*-isomer of citral, which elutes before geranial on polar columns (KINGSTON, 1962), constitutes about 33 per cent of the isomeric mixture. Citral was detected only in the extracts of the mandibular glands.

Mass spectroscopic analyses

The mass spectra of the two isomers of citral (neral and geranial) are illustrated in Figs. 1 and 2, along with the spectra of the two volatiles present in the mandibular glands of *T. subterranea* (Figs. 3, 4). All spectra were obtained under identical conditions in the gas chromatograph–mass spectrometer system. The mass spectra of the *T. subterranea* volatiles are completely congruent with those of both known isomers; peak 1 is identical to neral and peak 2 is identical to geranial.

The molecular ion of geranial is evident at m/e 152. High mass fragments correspond to losses of a methyl radical (m/e 137), a water molecule (m/e 134), and a

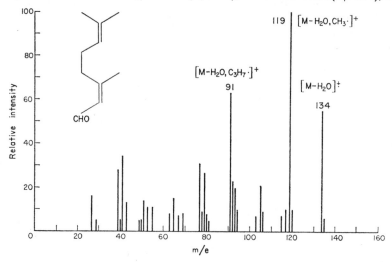

FIG. 1. The mass spectrum of neral.

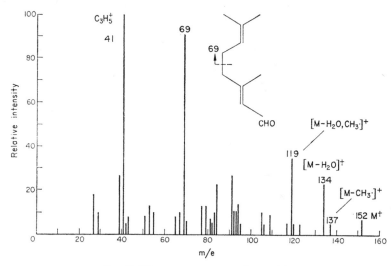

FIG. 2. The mass spectrum of geranial.

loss of both of these radicals (m/e 119) from the molecular ion (Fig. 2). The fragment of m/e 69 is probably formed by cleavage of the bond allylic to the two double bonds of geranial, a decomposition common in terpene hydrocarbons, alcohols, and

104

aldehydes having similar structures (RYHAGE and VON SYDOW, 1963; VON SYDOW, 1963, 1964). The fragment of m/e 41 is probably formed by the loss of ethylene from 69+ (RYHAGE and VON SYDOW, 1963).

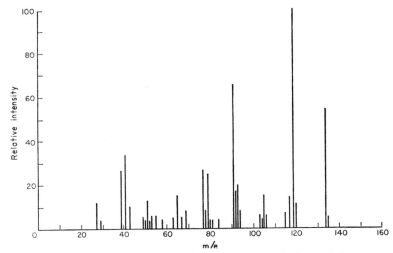

FIG. 3. The mass spectrum of *T. subterranea* volatiles, peak **1.**

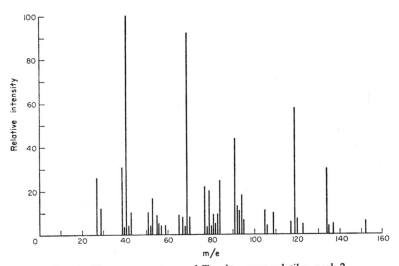

FIG. 4. The mass spectrum of *T. subterranea* volatiles, peak **2.**

The spectrum of neral shows no molecular ion (m/e 152). The intense peak at m/e 134 corresponding to a loss of 18 mass units and the predominance of peaks at m/e 91 and m/e 119 corresponding to further fragmentation of this ion (Fig. 1) indicate that the spectrum shown is largely that of the dehydrated species, $C_{10}H_{14}$. A mass spectrum of neral obtained by direct probe introduction into the ion source of the mass spectrometer was nearly identical to that of geranial, which suggests that the dehydration observed in the neral spectrum obtained by using the gas chromatograph interface was due to thermal effects in the gas chromatograph or in the interface rather than to electron impact.

Trail-laying behaviour of T. subterranea workers

The formation of a natural scent trail was observed by training workers to a sucrose solution which was located about 100 m from the nest. Workers of *T. subterranea* scattered their scent spots in an irregular pattern and the distances between consecutive scent spots were highly variable. The first spot was usually placed on the food source and the second mark was generally deposited about 30 to 50 cm from the food but often in a direction opposite to that of the nest. The third scent mark was placed about 4 to 5 m from the original mark and always in the direction of the nest. Subsequent scent depositions were placed from 1 to 5 m apart as the scout bee layed its scent trail toward the hive. The marking pattern which identified a given scent trail was characteristic of the bee which layed it.

It should be noted that when a recruit approached a bee marking a food source, the former flew toward the latter with its jaws open as if it were going to bite. Possibly, a recruit's habit of lightly grasping sticks treated with a trace of citral may represent an exaggeration of this mandible-spreading response normally observed in the field.

Reaction of T. subterranea workers to citral

Several workers were trained to a sucrose solution which was contained in an inverted Petri dish which was mounted on a glass platform. A small block was treated with a very small droplet of citral and placed on the Petri dish. The first bee arriving at the feeding platform was immediately attracted to the block which it approached directly and then proceeded to grasp lightly. After releasing the block, the bee then crawled to the syrup and fed. During the next 30 min this ritual was repeated without variation by 12 additional workers. In no instance did any of the workers exhibit any apparent aggressive behaviour.

In a second experiment, blocks treated with a small droplet of citral were placed on one side of the feeding platform and the number of bees which alighted on the side of the platform containing the treated block was recorded. The platform was rotated 90 and 180° in order to avoid learning responses. Workers made 40 visits to the feeding station and in all 40 cases the bees landed in the proximity of the citral-treated block.

In a third experiment, the closely related terpene citronellal was substituted for citral. *T. subterranea* workers appeared to be completely indifferent to the treated blocks and no attraction was evident. Workers of *T. droryana* which were collecting the sucrose solution at the same time, showed no response to either the citral- or the citronellal-treated blocks.

106

Significantly, workers of *T. subterranea* orient to citral when they are flying between food sources and the nest. When citral-impregnated blocks were placed on the ground midway between the nest and a feeding platform 80 cm away, the bees interrupted their flight in order to alight on the blocks.

In another series of experiments, blocks which were thoroughly impregnated with citral were placed inside the nest opening of a *T. subterranea* nest. Workers immediately attacked the block by gripping it and shaking it with their mandibles. The agitated workers moved rapidly and erratically in the hive but they made no attempt to fly out of the nest entrance. Frequently, the workers locked their mandibles on the treated block and hung tenaciously onto this object.

The reactions of bee species to citral

Trigona subnuda. After a citral-impregnated block was placed inside the nest, the workers became greatly agitated. Field bees flew out of the nest and did not return for over 20 min. The majority of the bees moved frenetically around the nest but avoided any contact with the treated block. Some of the older bees bit the block but immediately recoiled from the target object. The queen retreated from the brood area for about 10 min.

Trigona droryana. The reactions of the workers were virtually identical to those of *T. subnuda* workers. After introduction of the treated block, organized activity in the colony virtually ceased. Many workers flew out of the nest entrance and would not re-enter for the duration of the test. Several bees attempted to bite the block but, in general, the excited workers avoided the area proximate to the citral source. Total colonial disruption was evident for at least 10 min after the block was removed.

Trigona testaceicornis. The reactions of workers of this species were identical to those of *T. droryana*, if not even more exaggerated. Organized colonial activity ceased as soon as the citral-impregnated block was introduced into the nest.

Trigona varia. Initially, the workers became very agitated when the terpene-treated block was introduced. However, within 3 to 4 min, workers approached the block and began to cover it with resin. In about 20 min, the block was thoroughly coated with resin. If a citral-treated source was placed in front of the nest entrance, workers flew out in large numbers and aggressively attacked it with their mandibles.

Trigona postica. In general, the workers became very active subsequent to the introduction of the terpene into the nest. However, bees in the brood area remained undisturbed. Many workers haltingly attempted to remove the citral source and this operation took about 40 min to achieve. When a citral-treated source was placed outside the nest entrance, the excited workers began to fan intensely and a large number of bees formed at the nest opening with their abdomens directed at the block.

Melipona quadrifasciata. Citral, when placed near the nest entrance, caused a total breakdown in colonial activity. In some nests the workers milled excitedly about in the nest but did not fly out. In other cases, many workers immediately evacuated the nest and did not return until the terpenoid source had been removed.

Melipona rufiventris. No demonstrable reaction to citral was evident.

Apis mellifera adansonii. Citral appeared to act as a mild repellent to workers of this subspecies. In several instances workers approached the treated block, bit it, and then walked away.

Bombus atratus. Workers of this aggressive species appeared to be slightly repelled by high concentrations of citral.

DISCUSSION

The chemical basis of insect sociality must be interpreted both in terms of the identities of the pheromonal releasers and their parsimonious utilization in the social milieu. The rôles of citral in the biologies of several Hymenoptera illustrate clearly how the same compound may subserve either the same or different functions in different insects. Among ants, citral is produced in the mandibular glands of the formicine *Acanthomyops claviger* (Roger) (CHADHA et al., 1962) and the myrmicine *Atta sexdens* (L.) (BUTENANDT et al., 1959). This terpene is utilized both as an alarm releaser and defensive secretion by *A. claviger* (GHENT, 1961), whereas in *A. sexdens* citral appears to function solely as a defensive substance and alkyl ketones are utilized to communicate alarm (BLUM et al., 1968). However, it is chiefly among the social bees that citral has been exploited in order to expand the dimensions of sociality.

Citral is one of the components produced in the Nassanoff gland secretion of the honey bee (WEAVER et al., 1964; SHEARER and BOCH, 1966). This abdominal gland often is exposed and its volatiles liberated when workers are signalling the location of a food source. Citral appears to be the most potent attractant in the Nassanoff secretion (BUTLER and CALAM, 1969) and it is very probable that this terpene is utilized as an attractant for several types of unrelated social interactions. However, citral does not appear to function as an alarm releaser in the honey bee. As in citral-producing ants, a chemical releaser of alarm is present in the mandibular glands of *Apis* (SHEARER and BOCH, 1965) and, in addition, another potent alarm pheromone is produced in tissue associated with the sting (BOCH et al., 1962).

Among the stingless bees, citral is known only from species in two unrelated genera, *Trigona* and *Lestrimelitta*. The present report of the identification of the two isomers of citral in *T. subterranea* may indicate that other members of the subgenus *Geotrigona* also produce this terpene. On the other hand, we have not been able to detect this aldehyde in *Trigona* species in any other subgenera which we have examined and at this juncture it appears possible that citral is characteristic solely of species in the subgenus *Geotrigona*. The probable selective advantage to species in this subgenus of utilizing citral as a trail pheromone becomes evident when the rôles of this terpene in the biology of *T. subterranea* are appraised critically.

Citral must be regarded as the primary trail pheromone employed by *T. subterranea* workers. The two stereoisomers of the oxygenated terpene constitute about 95 per cent of the detectable volatiles present in the mandibular gland secretion, the source of the trail pheromone of this species. Citral acts as a powerful attractant for *T. subterranea* workers and based on our observations we consider this aldehyde the best attractant for a species of bee that we have ever observed. We have not found citral to be attractive to stingless bees in any other subgenera; species other than *T. subterranea* which visited feeding platforms on which were located citral-treated sticks appeared to be indifferent or even repelled by this terpene. Thus, it is possible that the citral-fortified scent trails laid by workers of *T. subterranea* are quite specific for workers of this species and perhaps other species in the subgenus *Geotrigona*. Chemical and behavioural studies on the mandibular gland secretions of sympatric species of *Geotrigona* will be required in order to determine how trail competition is reduced in species with overlapping distributions.

The specificity of *T. subterranea* for citral implies a high degree of olfactory acuity on the part of workers of this species. That this is indeed the case is indicated by the failure of citronellal to act as a surrogate for citral. Citral and citronellal are aldehydic terpenes which differ only by one double bond. Since these two oxygenated compounds boil within 22°C of each other, it is obvious that vapour pressure cannot be considered as a major factor which contributes to the selective sensitivity of *T. subterranea* workers to citral. Ultimately, the specific chemical 'language' which citral constitutes for workers of *T. subterranea* may reflect the ability of these bees to selectively decode the information carried by this acyclic monoterpene after it has reacted with the complementary olfactory sites on the antennae.

Citral is also an alarm pheromone for *T. subterranea* workers and high concentrations of this aldehyde will frequently release attack behaviour. Presumably, high concentrations will result when substantial numbers of workers discharge the contents of their mandibular glands in a localized area. Usually, this situation would occur proximate to or in the nest at a time of possible colonial jeopardy. Thus, the momentary aggressive propensities of the workers would be directed toward any alien animal in the environment of the nest. Since an alarm signal can be generated by the same compound that functions as a trail pheromone, workers of *T. subterranea* have increased their information output without requiring any increase in their natural products repertory. Such pheromonal parsimony appears to be common among the Hymenoptera and must be considered a key factor in the development of invertebrate sociality.

The rôles of citral in the biology of *L. limao* illustrate vividly how a pheromone has been exploited in order to achieve a *modus vivendi* which has diverged considerably from the mainstream of meliponine behaviour. Workers in the genus *Lestrimelitta* lack corbiculae and, as a consequence, must rob in order to obtain sufficient protein-based food to survive. Food is obtained by robbing the nests of other species of stingless bees and the citral-dominated mandibular gland secretion plays a major if not key rôle in the entire robbing operation. MOURE *et al.* (1956) reported that when a few scout bees locate a suitable nest, they are probably killed in the entrance and in the process the contents of their hypertrophied mandibular glands (COSTA CRUZ, 1962) are evacuated. Citral pervades the nest and simultaneously diffuses into the air and functions to attract more *Lestrimelitta* workers which begin to raid. It has been emphasized that workers of the host species become rapidly disoriented and sustained resistance to the plundering *Lestrimelitta* workers ceases (MOURE *et al.*, 1956). It now appears certain that the breakdown in cohesive social behaviour which characterizes the reaction of a species under attack results from the powerful stimulative effect produced by the citral which has permeated the interior of the nest.

The reactions to citral of three species of meliponines, *T. droryana*, *T. testaceicornis*, and *M. quadrifasciata*, were characterized by a complete disruption in social organization as long as the terpene was present. Field and guard bees, those which normally defend the nest from predators, abandoned the colony and flew to the exterior during the time when citral permeated the hive. These three species normally are robbed by *Lestrimelitta*. Their over-reactive responses to citral are remarkably similar to their reactions when their nest has been invaded by workers of *L. limao*. On the other hand, we have observed that meliponines such as *T. varia*, *T. postica*, and *T. rufiventris*, species which are not known to be raided by *Lestrimelitta*, react mildly to citral and appear to be quite capable of defending their nests when this terpene is present in high concentrations. Thus, citral effectively disarms those species whose nests are normally plundered by *Lestrimelitta* workers. In one sense this has selective value for both the victims and the attackers since mortality on either side is negligible during *Lestrimelitta* raids (MOURE *et al.*, 1956). However, the ability of *Lestrimelitta* to exploit a pheromone in order to neutralize the defensive activities of another species may not be a raiding adaptation which is limited to bees.

Ant species in several genera keep slave ants which are obtained by raiding the colonies of the slave species. The raids of *Formica sanguinea* Latr. and *Polyergus* species are characterized by a rapid breakdown in resistance on the part of the host species like that which occurs during *Lestrimelitta* raids. BERGSTRÖM and LÖFQVIST (1968) have identified the constituents present in the Dufour's gland of the slave raiders *F. sanguinea* and *Polyergus rufiescens* (Latr.) and their slaves *Formica fusca* L. and *Formica rufibarbis* F. The hypertrophied Dufour's glands of the slave-keeping species contain compounds which are capable of releasing alarm behaviour in *Formica* species (MASCHWITZ, 1964). We suspect that, as in *Lestrimelitta*, pheromones secreted by raiding ants may be primarily responsible for the breakdown in resistance which characterizes the behaviour of the host workers in raided nests. The dissolution of organized social behaviour which occurs when certain species of ants are exposed to high concentrations of alarm pheromones almost guarantees that they will be incapable of maintaining sustained resistance to the raiding ants. Similarly, in *Conomyrma pyramicus* (Roger) workers will not enter their nests when their alarm pheromone is present in high concentrations (BLUM and WARTER, 1966), a behavioural response that we have already noted in the species of *Trigona* that are susceptible to *Lestrimelitta* raids. We believe that subsequent research on the basis of slave-raiding in ants will demonstrate that this phenomenon is predicated on the use of highly stimulatory odorants on the part of the attacking formicids.

Although citral is a potent pheromone for workers of *Lestrimellitta*, it would be incorrect to classify this compound as a pheromone for the *Trigona* species which are raided. The frenetic reactions of raid-susceptible *Trigona* species after exposure to citral confers an obvious adaptative advantage to the attacking bees. It seems appropriate to regard citral as an allomone as well as a pheromone for *Lestrimelitta* workers. BROWN (1968) has defined an allomone as a substance possessed by a species which, when perceived by another species, produces a reaction in the latter which is favourable to the transmitter. Although Brown had exemplified his definition with glandular secretions whose favourable gustatory or olfactory qualities pacify workers of the host species, it requires only a slight broadening of the definition to encompass those secretions which produce a frenetic response on the part of the receiver species. Thus, citral can be regarded as both a pheromone and an allomone when this terpene is being utilized during raids.

Citral emerges as one of a probable host of compounds whose communicative functions vary with different species. In *T. subterranea*, it represents the first hymenopterous trail pheromone to be identified, but, in addition, it also functions as an alarm pheromone and local attractant. *L. limao* also utilizes citral as a pheromone, but, in addition, this aldehyde is employed to excessively stimulate a raided species and thus to effectively eliminate the defensive reactions of the host workers. The versatile utilization of citral by meliponines emphasizes further that many of the foundations of insect sociality are comprehensible in terms of the behavioural plasticity of insects in the presence of their chemical communicative stimuli.

Acknowledgements—A travel grant to Brazil was provided by a co-operative agreement between M. S. B. and the U.S. Department of Agriculture. We thank the Fundação de Amparo á Pesquisa de Estado de São Paulo for generous support.

REFERENCES

BERGSTRÖM G. and LÖFQVIST J. (1968) Odour similarities between the slave-keeping ants *Formica sanguinea* and *Polyergus rufescens* and their slaves *Formica fusca* and *Formica rufibarbis*. *J. Insect Physiol.* **14**, 995–1011.

BLUM M. S. (1966) Chemical releasers of social behavior—VIII. Citral in the mandibular gland secretion of *Lestrimelitta limao* (Hymenoptera: Apoidea: Melittidae). *Ann. ent. Soc. Am.* **59**, 962–964.

BLUM M. S., PADOVANI F., and AMANTE E. (1968) Alkanones and terpenes in the mandibular glands of *Atta* species. *Comp. Biochem. Physiol.* **26**, 291–299.

BLUM M. S. and WARTER S. L. (1966) Chemical releasers of social behaviour—VII. The isolation of 2-heptanone from *Conomyrma pyramica* (Hymenoptera: Formicidae: Dolichoderinae) and its *modus operandi* as a releaser of alarm and digging behavior. *Ann. ent. Soc. Am.* **59**, 774–779.

BOCH R., SHEARER D. A., and STONE B. C. (1962) Identification of *iso*-amyl acetate as an active component of the sting pheromone of the honey bee. *Nature, Lond.* **195**, 1018–1020.

BROWN W. L. (1968) An hypothesis concerning the function of the metapleural glands in ants. *Am. Nat.* **102**, 188–191.

BUTENANDT A., LINZEN B., and LINDAUER M. (1959) Über einen Duftstoff aus der Mandibledrüse der Blattschneiderameise *Atta sexdens rubropilosa* Forel. *Arch. Anat. micr. Morph. exp.* **48**, 13–19.

111

Butler C. G. and Calam D. H. (1969) Pheromones of the honey bee—The secretion of the Nassanoff gland of the worker. *J. Insect Physiol.* **15**, 237–244.

Chadha M. S., Eisner T., Monro A., and Meinwald J. (1962) Defense mechanisms of arthropods—VII. Citronellal and citral in the mandibular gland secretions of the ant *Acanthomyops claviger* (Forel). *J. Insect Physiol.* **8**, 175–179.

Costa Cruz C. da (1962) Anatomia e histologia comparadas das glândulas mandibulares dos Meliponideos. *Archos Mus. nac., Rio de J.* **52**, 79–84.

Ghent R. L. (1961) Adaptive refinements in the chemical defense mechanisms of certain Formicinae. Doctoral Dissertation, Cornell University, Ithaca, New York.

Kingston B. H. (1962) A fresh look at citral. *Mfg Chem.* **33**, 510–512, 514, 518.

Lindauer M. and Kerr W. E. (1958) Die gegenseitige Verständigung bei den stachellosen Bienen. *Z. vergl. Physiol.* **41**, 405–434.

Lindauer M. and Kerr W. E. (1960) Communication between the workers of stingless bees. *Bee Wld* **41**, 29–41, 65–71.

Maschwitz U. (1964) Gefahrenalarmstoffe und Gefahrenalarmierung bei sozialen Hymenopteren. *Z. vergl. Physiol.* **47**, 596–655.

Moure J. S., Nogueira-Neto P., and Kerr W. E. (1956) Evolutionary problems among the Meliponinae. *Proc. int. Congr. Ent.* **2**, 481–493.

Ryhage R. and Von Sydow E. (1963) Mass spectrometry of terpenes—I. Monoterpene hydrocarbons. *Acta chem. Scand.* **17**, 2025–2035.

Shearer D. A. and Boch R. (1965) 2-Heptanone in the mandibular gland secretion of the honey-bee. *Nature, Lond.* **206**, 530.

Shearer D. A. and Boch R. (1966) Citral in the Nassanoff pheromone of the honey bee. *J. Insect Physiol.* **12**, 1513–1521.

Von Sydow E. (1963) Mass spectrometry of terpenes—II. Monoterpene alcohols. *Acta chem. Scand.* **17**, 2504–2512.

Von Sydow E. (1964) Mass spectrometry of terpenes—III. Monoterpene aldehydes and ketones. *Acta chem. Scand.* **18**, 1099–1104.

Weaver N., Weaver E. C., and Law J. H. (1964) The attractiveness of citral to foraging honeybees. *Prog. Rept.* **2324**, Texas A & M University.

Use of Pheromones as Insect Lures and
in Insect Control

Hexalure, an Insect Sex Attractant Discovered by Empirical Screening

N. Green, M. Jacobson and J. C. Keller

Chemical attractants have become an indispensable tool in the detection[1] and control[2] of certain destructive insect pests. The sex attractants emitted by the virgin females of several species of Lepidoptera have been shown to be C_{12-16} alkenol acetates[3,4]. Isolation and identification of minute amounts of natural lure is an arduous, often frustrating task, and we therefore undertook to supplement our isolation program with a search for new insect attractants by a strictly empirical approach.

A large number of C_{12}, C_{14} and C_{16} alken-1-ol acetates were synthetized and evaluated as attractants for several insect species. One of these, *cis*-7-hexadecen-1-ol acetate, has proved to be an outstanding attractant for male pink bollworm moths, *Pectinophora gossypiella* (Saunders), eliciting a copulatory response in laboratory tests and luring large numbers to field traps. As such, it becomes the first sex attractant to be discovered by empirical means. The attractiveness of this compound, which we have named hexalure, is highly unusual, since propylure[4], the natural pink bollworm sex pheromone, is a C_{16} alkadienol acetate which has a branched chain and *trans* configuration.

Hexalure is far more attractive than propylure, which requires admixture with an activator[5] before it can lure males in the field. In tests with several species of insects, hexalure attracted only the pink bollworm, and this insect was not attracted to the *trans* isomer of hexalure.

Hexalure was synthetized by first condensing 2-(7-octynyloxy)-tetrahydropyran[6] with 1-bromooctane, according to previously published procedures[7], to give a 40% yield of 2-(7-hexadecynyloxy)-tetrahydropyran (bp, 140–145 °C at 0.001 mm Hg; n_D^{25}, 1.4636). This product was refluxed with acetic acid-acetyl chloride[6,7] to give a quantitative yield of 7-hexadecyn-1-ol acetate (bp, 117–121 °C at 0.001 mm; n_D^{25}, 1.4532), which was semihydrogenated to the desired product. Hexalure (bp, 100–104 °C at 0.001 mm, 121.5–124.5 °C at 0.08–0.14 mm; n_D^{25}, 1.4484) is a clear, colorless liquid with a mild odor reminiscent of freshly cut grass. Analysis of one lot by a new gas chromatographic method[8] showed the isomeric composition to be roughly 80% *cis* and 20% *trans*.

The efficacy of *cis*-7-hexadecen-1-ol acetate as an attractant for pink bollworm moths was evaluated in laboratory and field tests at Brownsville, Texas, and Phoénix, Arizona. In a preliminary test, a trap baited with 6 mg of hexalure caught, during 7 days, 51% of the male moths caught by the natural sex attractant extracted from 25 virgin females. Over a 14-day period the synthetic/natural catch ratio was 42%. In extensive field tests 60 mg of hexalure was initially about equal to 50 female equivalents of natural lure but after 5–7 days the synthetic lure at all test dosages was superior to either natural lure or to live caged virgin female moths.

Hexalure is now being used by the U.S. Department of Agriculture's Plant Pest Control Division to combat the pink bollworm in Florida and several southwestern states. It has been found to be more stable, more convenient to use, and much more economical than the previously used lure, which is a crude methylene chloride extract of the terminal abdominal segments of virgin female moths.

[1] M. JACOBSON, *Insect Sex Attractants* (Interscience Publishers, Inc., New York 1965), p. 104.

[2] M. JACOBSON, *Insect Sex Attractants* (Interscience Publishers, Inc., New York 1965), p. 112. – L. K. GASTON, H. H. SHOREY and C. A. SAARIO, Nature *213*, 155 (1967).

[3] R. S. BERGER, Ann. ent. Soc. Am. *59*, 767 (1966). – A. A. SEKUL and A. N. SPARKS, J. econ. Ent. *60*, 1270 (1967). – W. L. ROELOFS and H. ARN, Nature *219*, 513 (1968).

[4] W. A. JONES, M. JACOBSON and D. F. MARTIN, Science *152*, 1516 (1966).

[5] W. A. JONES and M. JACOBSON, Science *159*, 99 (1968).

[6] N. GREEN, M. JACOBSON, T. J. HENNEBERRY and A. N. KISHABA, J. med. Chem. *10*, 533 (1967).

[7] D. WARTHEN and M. JACOBSON, J. med. Chem. *10*, 1190 (1967); D. WARTHEN and M. JACOBSON, J. med. Chem. *11*, 373 (1968); D. WARTHEN, J. med. Chem. *11*, 371 (1968).

[8] D. WARTHEN and N. GREEN, J. Am. Oil Chem. Soc. *46*, 191 (1969).

Sex Pheromone of the Pink Bollworm Moth: Biological Masking by Its Geometrical Isomer

Martin Jacobson

Abstract. *A mixture of the* cis *and* trans *forms of propylure (10-propyl-*trans-*5,9-tridecadienyl acetate), the sex pheromone of the female pink bollworm moth, has been separated into its pure isomers by thin-layer chromatography. The* cis *isomer inhibits or masks the activity of the* trans *isomer, as little as 15 percent of the* cis *isomer being sufficient to completely nullify the activity of the* trans *isomer.*

In 1966, the sex pheromone produced by the female pink bollworm moth, *Pectinophora gossypiella* (Saunders), was isolated, identified, and synthesized (*1*). The compound, which was shown to be 10-propyl-*trans*-5,9-tridecadienyl acetate (structure I) and was designated "propylure," elicits a high degree of sexual excitement, including copulatory attempts, among caged male moths exposed to it in the laboratory.

$$CH_3CH_2CH_2$$
$$|$$
$$C{=}CH(CH_2)_2CH{=}CH(CH_2)_4OCCH_3$$
$$|$$
$$CH_3CH_2CH_2 \qquad \overset{\|}{O}$$

I

Eiter *et al.* (*2*) prepared propylure by a different method and reported that it showed no activity, although the details of their biological tests were not given (*3*). They concluded that propylure is not the pink bollworm sex pheromone, despite the fact that their preparation was admittedly geometrically impure. Active propylure prepared in our laboratories was a pure single isomer (*trans*), and this prompted me to investigate their preparation in an effort to explain the contradiction.

An explanation for the lack of activity appeared to be a possible masking effect caused by isomers admixed with propylure in the preparation of Eiter *et al.* Although these investigators discount a masking phenomenon as a factor in pheromone inhibition or inactivation (*2*), authentic cases of pheromone masking by admixed contaminants have already been reported

116

for the sex pheromones of the gypsy moth, *Porthetria dispar* (L.) *(4)*, introduced pine sawfly, *Diprion similis* (Hartig) *(5)*, corn earworm, *Heliothis zea* (Boddie) *(6)*, tobacco budworm, *H. virescens* (F.) *(6, 7)*, American cockroach, *Periplaneta americana* (L.) *(8)*, cynthia moth, *Samia cynthia* (Drury) *(9)*, cabbage looper, *Trichoplusia ni* (Hübner) *(10)*, and omnivorous leaf roller, *Platynota stultana* (Walsingham) *(11)*. In the case of *Trichoplusia ni*, whose sex pheromone is *cis*-7-dodecenyl acetate *(12)*, the agent responsible for masking is the corresponding *trans* isomer. This is likewise true for gyplure (12-acetoxy-*cis*-9-octadecen-1-ol), a synthetic sex attractant for the gypsy moth, which is completely inactivated by admixture with 20 percent of its *trans* isomer *(13)* or even smaller amounts of ricinoleyl (*cis*) alcohol *(14)*.

Eiter *et al.* *(2)* reported that their preparation of propylure was a 1:1 mixture of the *cis* and *trans* isomers, and it therefore seemed highly likely that the activity of the latter was being completely inhibited by the former isomer. That this was indeed the case has now been shown by preparing propylure according to the exact procedure described by Eiter and co-workers *(2)*, separating the resulting mixture into its geometrical isomers, and testing them alone and in combination for activity on male pink bollworm moths.

The propylure obtained by Eiter's procedure was a colorless liquid [b.p., 130° to 135°C at 0.1 mm-Hg; n_D^{25} 1.4610; Eiter *et al.* *(2)* reported b.p., 90° to 100°C at 0.05 mm; n_D^{20} 1.4612] whose gas-liquid chromatogram *(15)* showed one major and one minor component with retention times of 13.5 and 12.5 minutes, respectively. The minor component, comprising approximately 10 percent of the mixture, was identi-fied as the isomeric 9-propyl-5,9-tridecadienyl acetate (*cis* and *trans*) as reported by Eiter *et al.* This contaminant was efficiently separated by slow distillation, at 0.1 mm-Hg pressure, through a spinning band column; it boiled at 129° to 131°C (n_D^{25} 1.4600), whereas the major component boiled at 134°C (n_D^{25} 1.4630).

The major component was readily separated into *cis* and *trans* forms of propylure by preparative thin-layer chromatography on silica gel impregnated with silver nitrate *(16)*. With benzene-hexane (80:20) as the developing solvent, the *cis* and *trans* isomers showed R_F values of 0.31 and 0.50, respectively; propylure prepared by the method of Jones *et al.* *(1)* showed R_F 0.51 under these conditions. The ratio of *cis* to *trans* isomer in the mixture was 40:60.

The infrared spectrum of the separated *trans*-propylure showed a medium band at 965 cm⁻¹ (*trans* HC=CH) that was absent in the spectrum of the *cis* isomer, and the compound exhibited a retention time of 13.7 minutes by gas-liquid chromatography. *cis*-Propylure showed an inflexion at 740 cm⁻¹ on its infrared spectrum and a chromatographic retention time of 13.2 minutes. The *cis* isomer could be converted readily into the *trans* isomer by ultraviolet irradiation of its hexane solution containing a trace of iodine.

Laboratory bioassays were conducted with the isomers and their mixtures by exposing caged male moths to the air from pipettes containing the vapors of their methylene chloride solutions *(1, 17)*. Of 100 males used in each test, approximately 75 showed sexual excitement when exposed to *trans*-propylure, whereas only 3 or 4 moths responded to *cis*-propylure, the isomeric 9-propyl-5,9-tridecadienyl acetate, or methylene chloride. Males exposed to the *trans* isomer within 15 minutes after exposure to the *cis* isomer failed to respond, but a complete response was obtained each time in consecutive exposures to the *trans* isomer alone. Vapors of *trans*-propylure containing 10 percent of the *cis* isomer elicited a response in only 15 percent of the moths, and mixtures containing at least 15 percent *cis* isomer failed to cause a response.

Thus, *cis*-propylure acts as an inhibitor or masking agent for *trans*-propylure, but the mechanism through which this occurs is not yet understood. Presumably, the vapors of the *cis* isomer act on the antennal sensory system to block temporarily the nerve endings responsible for sex pheromone detection.

References and Notes

1. W. A. Jones, M. Jacobson, D. F. Martin, *Science* 152, 1516 (1966).
2. K. Eiter, E. Truscheit, B. Boness, *Justus Liebig's Ann. Chem.* 709, 29 (1967).
3. It was subsequently learned, by personal communications from Dr. Karl Eiter, Bayerwerk-Leverkusen, Köln-Stammheim, West Germany, and Dr. Milton T. Ouye, U.S. Department of Agriculture, Brownsville, Texas, that the biological tests had been conducted with caged, laboratory-reared male moths by the usual laboratory test (*1*).
4. J. Prüffer, *Zool. Pol.* 2, 43 (1937); M. Beroza, *J. Econ. Entomol.* 60, 875 (1967).
5. J. E. Casida, H. C. Coppel, T. Watanabe, *J. Econ. Entomol.* 56, 18 (1963).
6. R. S. Berger, J. M. McGough, D. F. Martin, *ibid.* 58, 1023 (1965).
7. M. M. Martin, personal communication.
8. M. Jacobson and L. A. Smalls, *J. Econ. Entomol.* 59, 414 (1966).
9. ———, *ibid.* 60, 296 (1967).
10. H. H. Toba, personal communication.
11. R. M. Waters, personal communication.
12. R. S. Berger, *Ann. Entomol. Soc. Amer.* 59, 767 (1966).
13. M. Jacobson, *Advan. Chem.* 41, 1 (1963).
14. R. M. Waters and M. Jacobson, *J. Econ. Entomol.* 58, 370 (1965); for discussion of pheromone masking, see M. Jacobson, *Insect Sex Attractants* (Interscience, New York, 1965), 154 pp.
15. The chromatography was carried out on an F&M model 500 instrument equipped with a model 1609 flame-ionization attachment on stainless steel columns packed with 5 percent SE-30 on Chromosorb W (3.05 m by 0.31 cm) at 185°C; the nitrogen flow rate was 25 ml/min.
16. Adsorbosil-ADN-1, containing 10 percent calcium sulfate binder and 25 percent silver nitrate, obtained from Applied Science Laboratories, State College, Pennsylvania.
17. I thank Dr. H. M. Graham, U.S. Department of Agriculture, Brownsville, Texas, for supplying the insects used in the bioassay tests.

Physiology of Insect Pheromone Response

EFFECTS OF MALE AND FEMALE SCENT ON REPRODUCTIVE MATURATION IN YOUNG FEMALE *TENEBRIO MOLITOR*

GEORGE M. HAPP,   MARK E. SCHROEDER,   and JAMES C. H. WANG

Abstract—In the first 7–10 days after emergence from the pupal cuticle, oöcyte length and emission of sex attractant increase in female mealworm beetles. Shortly after ecdysis, females were isolated and exposed to one of three airstreams containing: (1) unscented air, (2) scent of mature males, and (3) scent of mature females. Within 3 days, females exposed to male scent exhibited greater growth of their terminal oöcytes and a higher level of sex pheromone emission than either of the other two groups. At 3 days, females exposed to female scent emitted significantly more sex attractant than those females in unscented air, but only at 7 days were significant effects of female scent reflected in oöcyte growth of isolated females. Apparently both male and female scents contain primer pheromones.

INTRODUCTION

WHEN in the vicinity of the opposite sex, it is of some advantage for an organism to be reproductively mature. In some species of insects, population density may influence the rate of maturation of individual members and thus may promote reproductive synchrony. The stimuli involved in these interactions are best understood for the desert locust, *Schistocerca gregaria*. Pheromones, produced by mature male locusts, accelerate sexual maturation in young adults (LOHER, 1961; HIGHNAM and LUSIS, 1962). In female mealworm beetles, *Tenebrio molitor*, both crowding and mating increase the rate of reproductive maturation. Oöcyte growth is more rapid in crowded females and in mated females, and the two influences are additive (MORDUE, 1965). Sex attractant is emitted at a higher titre by crowded virgins than by isolated ones (HAPP and WHEELER, 1969). It was the purpose of the present study to determine whether pheromones are responsible for these group effects in female *Tenebrio*.

PROCEDURE AND RESULTS

Tenebrio molitor were obtained from a stock culture and sexed in the pupal stage. Upon emergence from the pupal cuticle, each young female was placed in a 2 oz. glass jar, supplied with food and moisture (potato), and randomly assigned to one of three experimental groups. Series M females were exposed to the scent of 100 mature males; series F, to that of 100 mature females; and series C, the controls, to ambient laboratory air. For each group, air was pulled by water vacuum through a desiccator containing oatmeal and slices of potato (and the appropriate beetles for the M and F series) and then, via a system of rubber and glass tubing, through jars containing the isolated females. The isolated females were in parallel to one another; they were exposed only to the airstream from the desiccator and could not smell each other. In any set of experiments, all series were run simultaneously and thus all beetles were exposed to the same scent contaminants in the laboratory air.

Each group contained at least 7 females. After appropriate periods of exposure to the scent from the desiccators, the young females were removed from the airstream and the three groups compared in three respects: sex attractant emission, metabolic rate, and ovarian development.

Emission of sex attractant

Each young female was tested for attractiveness by bioassay on male beetles. For this bioassay procedure, 10 males were confined in a small Lucite chamber. While unscented air passed through the chamber, the males aggregated near the outflow end. When the airstream contained female scent, the males moved upwind and attempted to mount one another. The percentage of males responding varied with the potency of the scent (details in Happ and Wheeler, 1969).

Prior exposure to the scent of mature beetles enhanced sex attractant release in the young females. Both male and female scent produced this effect, and the influence of male scent was most dramatic. At 3 and at 7 days after ecdysis all three series were significantly different from one another (Table 1).

TABLE 1—PERCENTAGE OF MALES RESPONDING TO YOUNG FEMALES PREVIOUSLY EXPOSED TO MALE SCENT, FEMALE SCENT, OR AMBIENT AIR

Age of females (after emergence) (days)	M series	F series	C series
3		$\chi^2 = 44 \cdot 20, P < 0 \cdot 005$	
	79·7%	56·2%	43·1%
	$\chi^2 = 20 \cdot 14, P < 0 \cdot 005$	$\chi^2 = 5 \cdot 51, P < 0 \cdot 025$	
7		$\chi^2 = 22 \cdot 38, P < 0 \cdot 005$	
	85·7%	70·4%	56·3%
	$\chi^2 = 5 \cdot 02, P < 0 \cdot 025$	$\chi^2 = 5 \cdot 82, P < 0 \cdot 025$	

Metabolic rate

The metabolic rate of each young female was measured by Warburg respirometry (25°C, 2 hr). As shown in Table 2, there was no simple relationship between exposure to the scents and oxygen consumption at 3, 5, or 7 days. The only pattern which emerged from the data was a negative correlation ($R = -0.873$) between the number of full-term oöcytes and metabolic rate, i.e. when most ovarioles have completed the formation of the first oöcyte, the metabolic rate of these isolated virgins declines.

TABLE 2—RATE OF OXYGEN CONSUMPTION OF YOUNG FEMALES PREVIOUSLY EXPOSED TO MALE SCENT, FEMALE SCENT, OR AMBIENT AIR

Age of females (after emergence) (days)	$\mu l\ O_2$/mg per hr		
	M series	F series	C series
3	0.345 ± 0.0165	0.340 ± 0.009	0.313 ± 0.010
5	0.365 ± 0.0167	0.331 ± 0.034	0.427 ± 0.034
7	0.276 ± 0.055	0.291 ± 0.046	0.318 ± 0.058

Oöcyte growth

The extent of ovarian development was measured by combining the lengths of terminal oöcytes and ripe eggs in the left ovary (MORDUE, 1965). The scent of mature beetles accelerated ovarian growth (Fig. 1). At 3 days after emergence the terminal oöcytes of females of the M series were significantly larger ($P < 0.01$) than those of the other two series, whereas the F and C series were indistinguishable. By 4 days, a few ripe eggs had already appeared in the sac of the lateral oviduct of females in the M series. At 5 days, oöcyte length in the M series was greater than in the controls ($P < 0.01$) while beetles exposed to female scent were intermediate and were not significantly different from either. By 7 days, most females in both the M and F series had produced ripe eggs, but oöcyte length in the controls was only slightly greater than at 5 days.

DISCUSSION

On the basis of their mode of action, WILSON and BOSSERT (1963) have suggested that pheromones fall into two broad categories: the releasers and the primers. Releaser pheromones act primarily at the behavioural level by producing an immediate and reversible change in the behaviour of the recipient. In contrast, primer pheromones induce a more prolonged shift in the physiology of the recipient.

Tenebrio produces pheromones with at least three releaser effects on mating and oviposition (Fig. 2). The scent of adult females attracts and sexually excites the males (VALENTINE, 1931; TSCHINKEL *et al.*, 1967; HAPP and WHEELER, 1969). Male scent is attractive to females and releases oviposition behaviour (HAPP, 1969). Both of these pheromones act only on the opposite sex. The third releaser action

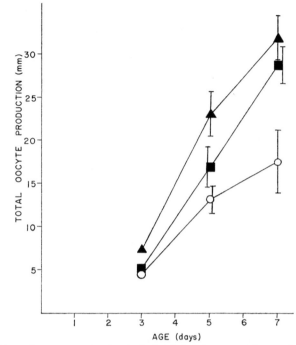

FIG. 1. Rate of oöcyte production in isolated females exposed to male scent, ▲; female scent, ■; ambient air, ○.

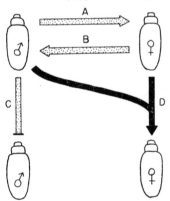

FIG. 2. Tentative representation of pheromones acting between male and female *Tenebrio molitor*. (A) Releaser produced by the male which attracts the female. (B) Releaser produced by the female which attracts and excites the male. (C) Releaser produced by the male which inhibits the response of other males to B. (D) Primers produced by both sexes which accelerate reproductive maturation in young females.

is antiaphrodisiac; male scent may inhibit the response of other males to the attractant produced by females. This inhibitory pheromone is emitted only in the presence of female scent, and some is transferred to the female during mating (HAPP, 1969). In addition to these releasers, the present study has shown that the scents of mature males and females have primer activity toward young virgin females. The site of pheromone synthesis in these beetles is not clear at present, but perhaps the sternal pit glands, which have been shown to be sexually dimorphic, are responsible for pheromone production (WIGGLESWORTH, 1948).

We do not know how many different molecules with pheromone activity are regulating reproduction in *Tenebrio*. The three releasers are distinct in their action and may be three separate molecules. On the other hand, two molecules could account for the releaser effects if one assumes that there is a pronounced increase in the emission of male pheromone when the males are exposed to female scent. Several possibilities are raised by the demonstration of primer activity in male and female scents. The fact that male scent was the more potent may suggest that the two sexes produce distinct primers of unequal potency. A simpler alternative is that one primer is emitted at differing rates in males and females. It is also conceivable that one or both of the attractants described earlier act as primers. Final resolution of these questions must await chemical identification of the pheromones involved.

Both oöcyte growth and emission of sex attractant are enhanced by the primer. Previous evidence indicates that these two phenomena are controlled by separate physiological regulatory mechanisms. MORDUE (1965) reported that the rate of oöcyte growth increased with crowding and mating and that eventually more ripe eggs were produced by crowded-mated females than by any other experimental group. In contrast, while isolated virgins produced the lowest titres of sex attractant and crowded virgins released much higher titres, the two parallel mated groups (crowded and isolated) were very similar to each other and fell in between these extremes (HAPP and WHEELER, 1969). In the case of oöcyte length, the measurement is a cumulative outcome of all the rates of growth over several days up to the point at which the beetle is dissected. The test for attractiveness towards males gives essentially an instantaneous rate, for it measures emission only during a test period of 5 min. Although these two aspects of reproductive physiology in the female appear to vary independently, the primer acts similarly on both—to increase the rate of the process. It might be added that the percentage of males responding to C series females is similar to that for isolated females and the response to F series females is similar to crowded virgin females described previously (HAPP and WHEELER, 1969). However, the M series females excited as many as 86 per cent of the males at 7 days. This level of pheromone emission has never been previously found in live females, and these data emphasize the very marked accelerating effect of male scent.

Acknowledgements—This study was supported by Grants CC-00285 and CC-00343 from the National Communicable Disease Center of the U.S. Public Health Service and by a grant from the Johnson Fund of the American Philosophical Society. LESLIE BROWN, KAREN SCHWEBER, and DAVID BRODHERSON assisted in beetle maintenance and the bioassays.

REFERENCES

HAPP G. M. (1969) Multiple sex pheromones of the mealworm beetle, *Tenebrio molitor* L. *Nature, Lond.* **222**, 180–181.

HAPP G. M. and WHEELER J. W. (1969) Bioassay, preliminary purification, and effect of age, crowding, and mating on the release of sex pheromone by female *Tenebrio molitor. Ann. ent. Soc. Am.* **62**, 846–851.

HIGHNAM K. C. and LUSIS O. (1962) The influence of mature males on the neurosecretory control of ovarian development in the desert locust. *Quart. J. micr. Sci.* **103**, 73–83.

LOHER W. (1961) The chemical acceleration of the maturation process and its hormonal control in the male of the desert locust. *Proc. R. Soc. Lond.* (B) **153**, 380–397.

MORDUE W. (1965) Studies on oöcyte production and associated histological changes in the neuro-endocrine system in *Tenebrio molitor* L. *J. Insect Physiol.* **11**, 493–503.

TSCHINKEL W., WILLSON C., and BERN H. A. (1967) Sex pheromone of the mealworm beetle (*Tenebrio molitor*). *J. exp. Zool.* **164**, 81–85.

VALENTINE J. M. (1931) The olfactory sense of the adult mealworm beetle *Tenebrio molitor* (Linn.). *J. exp. Zool.* **58**, 165–227.

WIGGLESWORTH V. B. (1948) The structure and deposition of the cuticle in the adult mealworm, *Tenebrio molitor* L. (Coleoptera). *Quart. J. micr. Sci.* **89**, 197–217.

WILSON E. O. and BOSSERT W. H. (1963) Chemical communication among animals. *Rec. Prog. Horm. Res.* **19**, 673–716.

Biosynthesis and Secretion of Pheromones in Insects

Epidermis and Pheromone Production in Males of the Desert Locust

L. STRONG

SYNCHRONOUS sexual maturation among crowded males of *Schistocerca gregaria* is achieved through a pheromone produced by the cells of the epidermis[1,2]. The synthesis and release of the pheromone have been correlated with marked histological changes which occur in the appearance of the epidermis during maturation[2]. I have examined the development of the epidermis in males of *S. gregaria*, and have found that the changes associated with maturation are more interesting than previously thought.

Desert locusts were reared under conditions described previously[3], and males were killed at various stages of adult life—from emergence to sexual maturity (28 days). The third abdominal tergite was fixed in Bouin's solution, embedded in ester wax (60° C), and sectioned at 10μ. The sections were stained with Mallory's triple stain.

As reported earlier[2,3], the epidermis of the newly ecdysed male has the appearance of a simple squamous epithelium: the cells are narrow and the nucleus occupies the majority of the cell. During the following 14 days the cells increase slightly in volume, an increase which seems to be associated with the completion of cuticle formation. Until the onset of sexual maturity the epidermis undergoes little modification. As sexual maturity advances, the integument assumes the characteristic yellow coloration, and the epidermis is transformed from a simple epithelium into a compound epithelium of large vacuolated cells, which earlier workers have interpreted in terms of elongation and vacuolation of the original epidermal cells[2,4]. This transformation is caused not by the alteration of the original epidermal cells, but by the appearance, growth and vacuolation of additional cells. Between the basement membrane and the original epidermal cells (Fig. 1*A*, cell 1) appear new cells (Fig. 1*B*, cell 2) which are clearly differentiated from the

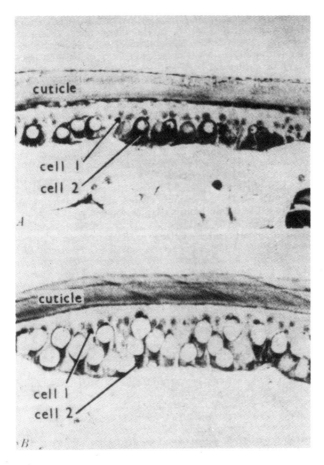

Fig. 1. Transverse sections of the third abdominal tergite of males of
S. gregaria. *A,* Male locust at the onset of maturity (16 days) showing
original epidermal cells (cell 1) and developing acidophils (cell 2). ×64.
B, Mature male locust (21 days) showing the acidophils with large
vacuoles. The acidophils are also lengthened, giving the epidermis a
multi-layered appearance. ×64. All material fixed in Bouin's solution
and stained with Mallory's triple stain.

original epidermal cells. The cytoplasm of the new cells
reacts strongly with the acid fuchsin part of Mallory's
stain, and they appear as deep-red cells among the neutral-
staining epidermal cells. The site of origin of the acidophils is not known, but they are not apparent in the
epidermis of the immature male. The vacuole appears
in the acidophil almost as soon as the cell itself can be
distinguished, and grows in the distal part of the cell,
pushing outwards into the epidermal cells which separate
the acidophils from the cuticle (Fig. 1A). The compound
layer of epidermal cells and acidophils increases greatly
in thickness largely as a result of the lengthening of the
acidophils. The overall volume of the cytoplasm decreases
as the vacuole grows, and the acidophils become drawn

out into thin columns with their vacuoles perched distally away from the basement membrane (Fig. 1B). In regions where the acidophils are very numerous many do not elongate—presumably as a result of competition from bordering cells—and the cytoplasmic stalk remains short. This creates the impression of a multi-layered epidermis of vacuolated cells (Fig. 1B). As the vacuole reaches its final volume the remaining cytoplasm of the acidophil is reduced to a thin band with the nucleus pressed against the vacuole. The result of the dramatic growth of the acidophils and their vacuoles is that the original epidermis is disorganized and compressed against the cuticle. The overall impression obtained by comparing only preparations of newly ecdysed males and fully mature males is that the original epidermal cells have become thickened and vacuolated[2,4]. In certain regions of the integument (for example, pleural folds) the acidophils do not appear, and the original epidermis remains as a well defined layer. It is interesting that Loher[2] observed two types of nuclei in the epidermis of mature males of S. gregaria: perhaps this can be explained in terms of the two cell types I have described.

In S. cancellata there are scent glands in the abdominal tergites of the mature male: these comprise a glandular cell and a duct cell, in addition to the normal epidermal cells[5]. It seems unlikely that the structures found in S. gregaria correspond to those in S. cancellata, while the integument of S. paranensis[6] seems to be identical with that of S. gregaria. Further work is being carried out on the integument of the male desert locust to clarify the site of origin of the acidophilic cells, and the mechanism by which the pheromone is released.

[1] Norris, M. J., *Anti-Locust Bull.*, 18 (1954).
[2] Loher, W., *Proc. Roy. Soc.*, 153, 380 (1960).
[3] Strong, L., *J. Exp. Biol.*, 48, 625 (1968).
[4] Chauvin, R., *Ann. Soc. Ent. Fr.*, 110, 133 (1941).
[5] Oglobin, A., *Arthropoda*, 1, 54 (1947).
[6] Strong, L., thesis (1964).

HORMONE–PHEROMONE RELATIONSHIPS IN THE BEETLE, *TENEBRIO MOLITOR*

MAYA MENON

Abstract—A study was undertaken to determine the rôle, if any, of the neuro-endocrine system in the production of a sex pheromone by adult females of *Tenebrio molitor*. The corpora allata, brain, the entire head, the frontal ganglion, or the ovaries were removed from newly emerged females. Ten to 14 days after the operation the pheromone content of these females was estimated in comparison with that of appropriate controls by biological assay. The pheromone activity of the extracts from females subjected to allatectomy and/or brain removal, or to decapitation, was significantly decreased when compared with sham-operated controls or normals. Reimplantation of the corpora allata or brain did not restore the pheromone level. However, treatment with juvenile hormone analogues was able to counter the effect of the operations. Removal of the frontal ganglion or the ovaries did not have any significant effect. The experimental results indicate that the secretion of the corpus allatum (juvenile hormone) is directly involved in the control of pheromone secretion; an intact brain–corpus allatum axis appears to be essential for normal production of pheromone by female *T. molitor*.

INTRODUCTION

HORMONAL control of sex pheromone production has been demonstrated by LOHER (1960) and NORRIS and PENER (1965) in males of *Schistocerca gregaria*, by BARTH (1961, 1962) and ROTH and BARTH (1964) in *Byrsotria fumigata*, by BARTH (1965) in *Pycnocilus surinaminus*, and by ZDAREK (1968) in the bug *Pyrrhocoris apterus*. Removal of corpora allata from female cockroaches (BARTH, 1962) and male locusts (LOHER, 1960) shortly after adult emergence results in failure of production of sex attractants as determined by male and female behaviour, respectively. Reimplantation of corpora allata (LOHER, 1960; BARTH, 1962) or injection of the juvenile hormone analogue, farnesyl methyl ether (FME), restores the capacity to produce pheromone in *B. fumigata* (BARTH and EMMERICH, 1968; EMMERICH and BARTH, 1968).

Despite these well-established examples, hormonal control of pheromone production does not seem to be a widespread phenomenon among insects. According to BARTH (1965), such a mechanism may be expected to occur only in those instances in which selection pressures favour its evolution. For example, in insects which have a long adult life and multiple reproductive cycles with periods in which mating is not possible, hormonal control of pheromone secretion is advantageous in bringing the two sexes together. On the other hand, insects which have a short, non-feeding adult life during which endocrine glands do not control egg maturation may not have need of hormone-controlled sex pheromone production. BARTH's (1965) comparative observations on two species of cockroaches and on two species of Lepidoptera with short, non-feeding adult stages concur with this scheme. If Barth's hypothesis extends to other orders of insects, *Tenebrio molitor* with its long adult life and repeated reproductive activity can be expected to have evolved a hormone-regulated mechanism of pheromone production.

A sex pheromone has been reported in female *T. molitor* (VALENTINE, 1931; TSCHINKEL *et al.*, 1967). TSCHINKEL *et al.* (1967) have further shown that the pheromone is secreted by both sexes, but appears to act as a sex excitant only on the males. However, according to AUGUST (1967) and HAPP (1969) the two pheromones are not identical and the male pheromone is attractive to females. As to the site of production of the pheromone, TSCHINKEL *et al.* (1967) reported that it is secreted from the surface of the metathoracic sternum and the first two anterior terga. The only indication that there might be a hormone–pheromone relationship in this species is the observation by TSCHINKEL *et al.* (1967) that release of the first ova coincides with the attainment of the plateau in pheromone level. The research reported here was undertaken to determine whether the endocrine system controls sex pheromone production in the females of the mealworm beetle, *T. molitor*.

MATERIALS AND METHODS

Rearing of insects

The *Tenebrio molitor* stock colony was maintained on wheat bran, lettuce, and water at room temperature in screen-topped steel containers. The pupae were collected, segregated according to sex, and kept in plastic Petri dishes. The emergents were separated every day. The pupae and adults of the two sexes were held separately in two light-controlled cabinets provided with an air circulation system. The temperature inside the cabinets averaged 26°C. The r.h. was about 60 to 70 per cent, and the photoperiod was regulated to 12 hr of light and 12 hr of darkness. The adult females used for the experiments were between 1 and 24 hr after emergence. The insects were maintained on bran and water if the experiments were run for 14 days, but were given water alone when the experiments were run for 10 days. The adult males were kept in separate boxes in the cabinet. They were routinely used as test animals in the bioassay 1 month or more after their emergence. Only vigorous individuals in good physical condition were used.

Surgical techniques

Ablation (removal of corpora allata, brain, frontal ganglion, or ovaries), implantation, ligation or decapitation, and treatment with hormones were performed on adult females.

Allactectomy. The paired corpora cardiaca and corpora allata are situated posterior and ventral to the brain and dorsal to the oesophagus. The newly emerged females were anaesthetized for 1 hr in water through which carbon dioxide was bubbled continuously. For the operation each insect was submerged in sterilized, insect saline (EPHRUSSI and BEADLE, 1936) in a Plasticine-lined Petri dish and secured in a prone position by Plasticine bands across the middle of the body. Under a binocular microscope, a small triangular flap of cuticle on the dorsal side of the head close to the neck membrane was excised with a small scalpel made from a fragment of a razor blade. The brain, tracheae, and fat body were thus exposed. The retrocerebral glands were located by removing the fat body by means of fine forceps and jets of insect saline. The corpora cardiaca and corpora allata are closely attached and had to be removed together. The bases of both corpora cardiaca were pulled free from their nervous connexions with the brain and other organs. Care was taken to minimize damage to tracheae. After the operation the cuticular flap was sealed into place, the saline drained off, and the wound daubed with a mixture of streptomycin and penicillin. The wound was dried with cotton wool and occasionally sealed with melted paraffin. The operated insects were placed in paper-lined plastic finger-bowls provided with screen tops and returned to the light-controlled cabinet. Insects treated identically, except that their corpora cardiaca and corpora allata were left untouched, served as sham-operated controls.

Brain removal. The head was operated upon as described above, exposing the brain. The optic peduncles were cut and the brain disconnected and carefully removed from the suboesophageal ganglion and corpora cardiaca–allata complex, and the wound treated as described above. In operated controls, after exposing the brain, the optic peduncles alone were cut to induce blindness.

Frontal ganglion removal. The frontal ganglion is located just anterior and ventral to the brain. A triangular window was cut on the dorsal side of the head as in the above two operations, exposing the ganglion and the brain. The ganglion was freed from its nervous connexions and removed. In some cases the recurrent nerve and the hypocerebral ganglion were also removed. Insects treated identically, except that the frontal ganglion was kept intact, served as controls.

Ligation or decapitation. The anaesthetized insect was ligated with thin cotton thread behind the head in order to isolate the thorax and abdomen from the influence of the neuroendocrine complex in the head. Several of the ligated insects were also decapitated the next day to ensure that the posterior part of the body would not receive any brain or corpora cardiaca–allata secretions. Normal (unoperated) insects served as controls.

Ovariectomy. The anaesthetized insect was submerged in saline and immobilized on its dorsum in a Plasticine-lined Petri dish by a strip of Plasticine. A rectangular window was cut into the ventral side of the last three abdominal segments, exposing part of the digestive and reproductive systems. The ovarian follicles with their ducts were carefully separated from the rest of the tissue and tracheae, the oviducts cut at their bases, and the two ovaries removed separately. In some operations the long filamentous spermathecal gland also was removed. Appropriate sham-operated controls were maintained.

Post-mortem examination. After extraction (see below) the insects were stored in 70% ethanol to record the number of mature oöcytes in the oviducts.

Hormone treatment

The juvenile hormone analogues, farnesyl methyl ether (FME) (Hoffman–LaRoche) and *trans,trans*-N,N-diethyl-3,7,11-trimethyl-10,11-epoxydodeca-2,6-dienamide (Syntex), were used to replace the corpora allata. Three solutions of FME were prepared in the following concentrations and solvents: 300 $\mu g/\mu l$ in olive oil, 145 $\mu g/\mu l$ in peanut oil, and 1 $\mu g/\mu l$ in acetone. Solutions of the Syntex compound were: 6 $\mu g/\mu l$ in olive oil, 10 $\mu g/\mu l$ in peanut oil, and 1 $\mu g/\mu l$ in acetone. Hormone solutions in oil were usually used for injection, whereas the solutions in acetone were used for external application. The syringe (10 μl) was rinsed several times in acetone and absolute ethanol after use. Insects usually received an injection or external application of 1 to 2 μl of the solutions. The first dose was given 1 day after the operation and the second was given 5 days after the first. Operated insects given only oil or acetone served as one set of controls, and sham-operated or normal insects without any treatment served as the second set of controls.

Biological testing

Because of the high sensitivity of the males, testing their responses to live females did not prove a satisfactory assay for pheromone estimation. For this reason, the biological assay developed by TSCHINKEL *et al.* (1967) was used. At the termination of the experiments all insects to be assayed were extracted individually (1 insect in 1 ml) for 18 to 24 hr in tetrahydrofuran (THF), freshly redistilled over KOH pellets. The insects were removed at the end of the extraction time, and the extracts were stored in screw-capped vials in a deep freeze. All solutions were tested within 1 to 2 weeks after extracting the insect in THF. When stored for a longer period the extracts gradually lost their activity.

For each test a random sample of 20 male beetles was taken and placed individually on clean wrapping paper under 100-mm Petri dishes. The tests were carried out in the darkroom under red light. The beetles were allowed to adapt to the new environment for about 5 min. Short pieces of glass rod, 3 mm in dia. and fire-polished at both ends, were washed in chromic acid and kept in ethanol until needed. They were wiped clean, dipped in the test solution to a uniform depth and placed on a small rack. One min after each glass rod was dipped, it was placed under a Petri dish containing a test beetle. The dipping was carried out at regular intervals keeping all time-intervals constant. Each test lasted for 20 min after the introduction of the glass rod. A copulation attempt was minimally defined as the male mounting the rod and bending the tip of its abdomen downward and anteriorly around the end of the rod (*cf.* Fig. 1a in TSCHINKEL *et al.*, 1967). After 20 min any beetle not having responded as described above was recorded as negative. This interval seemed adequate, for if the male was attracted to the extract on the glass rod, it generally gave a positive response within 1 to 5 min. Each extract was tested twice in this fashion. Test beetles were not used more than once per day.

Statistical analysis

To test the significance of differences among mean values of pheromone responses obtained from various experimental conditions, Barlett's test for homogeneity of variance (chi-square test) and the one-way analysis of variance procedure (STEEL and TORRIE, 1960) were performed. If a significant F ratio was obtained, Tukey's w procedure was used to determine which of the means were significantly different. In all tests the minimum significance level was set as $P < 0.05$. All calculations were done using the digital computer CDC 6400 at the Berkeley Campus Computer Center.

Alternate method for estimating the effect of treatment on pheromone activity of extracts

In an alternate method, pheromone activity equivalent to a response 50 per cent or greater is recorded as positive and lower than 50 per cent is recorded as negative, in studying the effectiveness of operations and treatments. This method is explained further in the section on results.

Conversion of pheromone activity into arbitrary units

TSCHINKEL *et al.* (1967) defined the value of 1 unit/ml to be a concentration of pheromone giving $x/n = 0.50$. Following his method the activity of extracts from insects after various treatments was converted into units and compared. The detailed procedure is given in the section on results.

RESULTS

The mortality rate was about 50 per cent among the experimental insects and about 30 per cent among controls. Those animals that survived remained active until the termination of the experiments (10 or 14 days).

Normal Pheromone Activity

The pheromone activity of the extracts of females 10 days after emergence maintained on water alone was not significantly different from that of well-fed normals (Table 1). Dissection of the extracted insects showed that the rate of oöcyte

TABLE 1—PHEROMONE ACTIVITY OF EXTRACTS OF WATER-FED AND BRAN-FED FEMALE *T. molitor* 10 days AFTER EMERGENCE

Treatment	n	x/n (mean $\pm$ S.E.$_m$)	Comparison of means
Insects maintained on bran and water	3	13.0 ± 0	N.S.*
Insects maintained on water alone	9	13.4 ± 0.7	

n = number of female insects extracted; x/n = number of positive responses/20 males.

* N.S., difference not significant ($P > 0.05$).

maturation was also the same in both groups. Nutrition as such does not appear to play a rôle in pheromone secretion and egg maturation, at least not before 10 days after adult emergence.

Experimental Manipulations

Experiments with corpora allata

Controls. Pheromone activity of sham-operated controls was not different from that of normal insects of the same age. However, the activity of extracts of controls 10 days after emergence was significantly greater than that of controls 14 days after emergence.

Effect of allatectomy. Extracts of female insects whose corpora cardiaca–allata were removed showed pheromone activity significantly lower than that of the controls. However, a few females caused high responses in males. Furthermore, the pheromone activity of extracts from experimentals 14 days after emergence was also significantly lower than that from experimentals 10 days after emergence. Accordingly, the two groups (10 days and 14 days after emergence, both experimentals and controls) were compared separately. Table 2 shows the bioassay

TABLE 2—PHEROMONE ACTIVITY OF THE EXTRACTS OF CONTROL AND ALLATECTOMIZED FEMALE
T. molitor, 14 days AFTER EMERGENCE

Treatment	n	x/n (mean $\pm$ S.E.$_m$)	Comparison of means
Controls (sham-operated)	12	$10 \cdot 5 \pm 1 \cdot 0$	$P < 0 \cdot 005$
Allatectomized	11	$5 \cdot 3 \pm 0 \cdot 7$	

n = number of female insects extracted; x/n = number of positive responses/20 males.

results of the extracts from control and operated insects 14 days after emergence. All further experiments in which the females were maintained on water alone were terminated within 10 days of operation, because if kept longer without bran the animals became cannibalistic. Table 3, A1 and A2, shows the significant difference in the pheromone activity of females 10 days after sham operation and allatectomy.

Allatectomy and reimplantation of corpora allata. Although allatectomized insects showed a decrease in their pheromone activity (as evidenced by a fall in male responses to extracts of allatectomized females), reimplantation of the pair of corpora cardiaca–allata immediately after their extirpation did not prevent the fall in pheromone level (Table 3, A3).

Allatectomy and treatment with juvenile hormone analogues. Injection or external application of juvenile hormone analogues dissolved in oil or acetone at least partially restored activity of allatectomized females. It is not clear at present whether injection or external application is more effective, or whether there is a dose–response relationship. Since the difference between the responses with the two analogues (using different concentrations) was not significant, the two sets of observations were combined (Table 3, A4).

Conclusions. These experiments indicate that allatectomy lowers pheromone level, that reimplantation of the corpora allata has no effect, and that treatment of operated insects with juvenile hormone analogues restores the pheromone level.

TABLE 3—PHEROMONE ACTIVITY OF FEMALE *T. molitor* 10 days AFTER EMERGENCE, AFTER VARIOUS TREATMENTS

	Treatment	n	x/n (mean $\pm$ S.E.$_m$)	Comparison of means
A1	Controls (sham-operated)	28	$13{\cdot}4 \pm 0{\cdot}6$	1 vs. 2 $P < 0{\cdot}01$
A2	Allatectomy	27	$7{\cdot}9 \pm 0{\cdot}6$	1 vs. 3 $P < 0{\cdot}01$
A3	Reimplantation of corpora allata	10	$8{\cdot}1 \pm 1{\cdot}0$	1 vs. 4 N.S.*
A4	Treatment with juvenile hormone analogues after allatectomy	18	$10{\cdot}8 \pm 0{\cdot}8$	2 vs. 3 N.S.
				2 vs. 4 $P < 0{\cdot}05$
				3 vs. 4 N.S.
B1	Controls (optic nerve cut)	23	$12{\cdot}8 \pm 0{\cdot}7$	1 vs. 2 $P < 0{\cdot}05$
B2	Brain removal	16	$8{\cdot}3 \pm 1{\cdot}4$	1 vs. 3 $P < 0{\cdot}01$
B3	Brain + corpora allata removal	24	$6{\cdot}8 \pm 0{\cdot}7$	1 vs. 4 $P < 0{\cdot}05$
B4	Reimplantation of brain after removal	10	$8{\cdot}2 \pm 1{\cdot}3$	1 vs. 5 N.S.
B5	Treatment with juvenile hormone analogue after brain removal	8	$9{\cdot}6 \pm 1{\cdot}5$	2 vs. 3 N.S.
				2 vs. 4 N.S.
				2 vs. 5 N.S.
				3 vs. 4 N.S.
				3 vs. 5 N.S.
				4 vs. 5 N.S.
C1	Controls (sham-operated)	6	$12{\cdot}3 \pm 0{\cdot}7$	N.S.
C2	Removal of ovary and spermathecal gland, or ovary alone	12	$12{\cdot}2 \pm 1{\cdot}3$	
D1	Controls (sham-operated)	10	$12{\cdot}8 \pm 1{\cdot}1$	N.S.
D2	Frontal ganglion removed	15	$12{\cdot}0 \pm 1{\cdot}0$	
E1	Controls (normal)	19	$13{\cdot}1 \pm 0{\cdot}7$	1 vs. 2 $P < 0{\cdot}01$
E2	Decapitated or head ligated	17	$7{\cdot}9 \pm 0{\cdot}8$	1 vs. 3 N.S.
E3	Treatment of decapitated or ligated insects with juvenile hormone analogues	26	$13{\cdot}3 \pm 0{\cdot}4$	2 vs. 3 $P < 0{\cdot}01$

* N.S., difference not significant ($P > 0{\cdot}05$).

Experiments with the brain

Controls. Extracts of controls whose optic nerves were cut gave pheromone activity similar to that of normals (Table 3, B1).

Brain removal. Pheromone activity of extracts of decerebrated females showed a significant drop (Table 3, B2).

Removal of brain and corpora allata. Ablation of both organs together further lowered the pheromone level of the extracts of the females from that seen when corpora allata or brain alone were removed (Table 3, B3).

Reimplantation of brain. Reimplantation of a brain into debrained insects did not restore the pheromone level to normal (Table 3, B4).

Removal of brain and treatment with juvenile hormone analogues. Juvenile hormone analogues slightly increased the pheromone activity of brainless insects, but the difference was not significant, possibly owing to the small sample size (Table 3, B5).

Conclusions. These experiments indicate that the brain also has some influence over pheromone secretion, although its rôle may be indirect. Treatment of brainless insects with juvenile hormone analogues was not significantly effective in restoring the pheromone level.

Ovariectomy experiments

Controls. Pheromone activity of sham-operated controls was similar to that of normals (Table 3, C1).

Ovariectomy. The possibility that the ovary may be involved in the control of the pheromone secretion was eliminated when extracts of females devoid of their ovary and spermathecal glands showed pheromone activity as high as that of sham-operated controls (Table 3, C2).

Conclusions. The experiment shows that the ovary has no control over pheromone activity.

Removal of frontal ganglion

Controls. Sham-operated controls showed normal pheromone activity (Table 3, D1).

Frontal ganglionectomy. This operation was performed because of the reports of other workers on the rôle of the frontal ganglion in feeding, secretion of neuro-hormones, and egg maturation, together with the fact that the removal of corpora allata and brain in the present experiments did not completely eliminate all traces of pheromone. However, removal of the ganglion with its connectives and hypo-cerebral ganglion did not significantly lower the pheromone activity of the extracts (Table 3, D2), although impaired yolk deposition was apparent (Table 5, D).

Conclusions. The experiments indicate that the frontal ganglion is not directly involved in pheromone production.

Ligation and decapitation experiments

Controls. Normal females without any operations served as controls in this case, and their extracts showed normal pheromone activity (Table 3, E1).

Ligation or decapitation. Since none of the extirpations yielded extracts with zero pheromone activity and since removal of the suboesophageal ganglion (another possible centre of control) without damaging or killing the insect proved impossible, the influence of the entire anterior complex was eliminated by ligating the head or

138

by decapitation. The headless insects survived very well and moved about actively for as long as 10 days, at which time the experiments were terminated. The extracts of these individuals gave responses which were no different from those insects without corpora allata or brain but significantly different from those of normal controls (Table 3, E2).

Decapitation and treatment with juvenile hormone analogues. Treatment with juvenile hormone analogues proved effective. The pheromone activities of the extracts of these hormone-treated insects and those of normals were almost identical (Table 3, E3).

Conclusions. The results of treatment of decapitated insects with juvenile hormone analogues indicate that it is the secretion of the corpus allatum that is directly involved in the control of pheromone production, although the brain with intact nervous connexions is necessary for the secretion or the release of material from the corpora allata.

The results of the various experiments are summarized in Fig. 1.

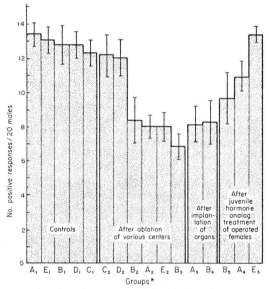

FIG. 1. Histogram showing pheromone activity 10 days after emergence of females of *T. molitor* after various treatments (vertical lines indicate S.E.$_m$). * See Table 3 for explanation of group numbers.

Evaluation of the Results of Various Treatments Using an Alternate Method

Since none of the operations resulted in extracts without pheromone activity, and since most extracts from normal insects showed pheromone activity above 50 per cent (x/n equal to or greater than 0·50), the data were evaluated by considering an activity of 50 per cent or above as positive and less than 50 per cent as negative. The percentages of female extracts giving positive responses, as thus defined, were tabulated (Table 4). Only a small number of extracts from females

TABLE 4—*T. molitor* SHOWING 'POSITIVE' PHEROMONE RESPONSES UNDER VARIOUS CONDITIONS

	Treatment	Fraction of females with pheromone activity above 50%	% Females with pheromone activity above 50%
A1	Controls (sham-operated)	30/40	75
A2	Allatectomy	6/38	15
A3	Reimplantation of corpora allata	3/10	30
A4	Treatment with juvenile hormone analogues after allatectomy	11/18	61
B1	Controls (optic nerve cut)	19/23	83
B2	Brain removal	4/16	25
B3	Brain + corpora allata removal	3/24	13
B4	Reimplantation of brain after removal	3/10	30
B5	Treatment with juvenile hormone analogue after brain removal	5/8	63
C1	Controls (sham-operated)	5/6	82
C2	Removal of ovary alone, or ovary with spermathecal gland	10/12	82
D1	Controls (sham-operated)	7/10	70
D2	Frontal ganglion removal	9/15	60
E1	Controls (normals)	16/19	84
E2	Decapitated or head ligated	4/17	24
E3	Treatment of decapitated or ligated insects with juvenile hormone analogues	24/26	92

devoid of their corpora allata, brain, or head gave positive responses. Reimplantation of corpora allata or brain did not raise the pheromone activity; however, treatment with juvenile hormone analogues was effective. Fig. 2 summarizes the occurrence of positive pheromone activity as defined above.

Estimation of Pheromone Activity in Units

An arbitrary unit of pheromone defined by TSCHINKEL *et al.* (1967) is the pheromone activity of 1 ml of extract resulting in a 50 per cent response in a group of 20 males. At first, the x/n ratios (positive responses/number of males tested) of two-, four-, eight-, sixteen-, thirty-two-, and sixty-fourfold dilutions (called dilution factors) of pheromone extract from normal females were plotted on semilog paper (Fig. 3). From this, the 'standard dilution factor' which resulted in

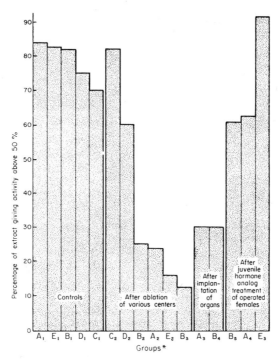

FIG. 2. Histogram showing pheromone activity above 50% in *T. molitor* females.
* See Table 4 for explanation of group numbers.

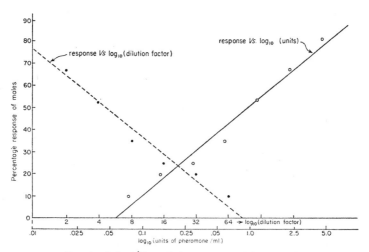

FIG. 3. Calculation of pheromone activity in units.

50 per cent response was read. Then, the different dilution factors of the normal extract were converted into units of pheromone by using the following equation

$$\frac{\text{Units of pheromone for a}}{\text{given response by males}} = \frac{\text{standard dilution factor}}{\text{dilution factor for that response}}.$$

These units were plotted on semi-log paper against male responses (Fig. 3). From this standard curve the pheromone concentrations in units of the extracts of the various experimental and control insects were obtained and tabulated (Table 5). When the unit values of pheromone in experimental and control groups are compared, it becomes obvious that the ablation of corpora allata, brain, or head reduces the content of pheromone in units to one-quarter to one-third that of controls and that hormone therapy is effective in doubling the pheromone activity in the operated insects.

TABLE 5—MEAN UNITS OF PHEROMONE/ml OF EXTRACTS OF INSECTS AFTER VARIOUS TREATMENTS

Treatment	Units/ml (mean)
Decapitated or ligated insects treated with juvenile hormone analogues	3·10
Controls (sham-operated) of experiment B, Table 3	3·00
Normals (unoperated)	2·40
Controls (optic nerve cut)	2·18
Controls (sham-operated) of experiment D	2·18
Controls (sham-operated) of experiment E	1·65
Ovariectomy	1·60
Frontal ganglionectomy	1·41
Juvenile hormone analogue treatment after allatectomy	1·26
Juvenile hormone treatment after brain removal	0·90
Brain removal	0·60
Brain reimplantation	0·60
Corpora allata reimplantation	0·59
Allatectomy	0·56
Ligation or decapitation	0·54
Brain + corpora allata removal	0·40

Correlation between Egg Maturation and Pheromone Secretion

Dissection of insects stored in ethanol after extraction revealed that one of the consequences of the removal of corpora allata, brain, or head is the inhibition of ovarian development. Those insects which showed mature eggs after these operations generally yielded extracts which gave high responses in males. However, there were instances where pheromone activity was high in insects without mature eggs and low in insects with mature eggs. Reimplantation of corpora allata or brain into operated insects did not restore the ability of the insects to develop mature eggs. Further, although treatment with juvenile hormone analogues in the concentrations used here did increase the pheromone level in operated females,

142

these compounds did not stimulate yolk deposition. Frontal ganglionectomy resulted in an apparent inhibition of egg maturation, although it did not significantly affect the pheromone level. Although juvenile hormone analogues can substitute for the neuroendocrine complex in inducing production of pheromone, an intact neuroendocrine complex seems to be essential for the induction of yolk deposition in the ovary of *T. molitor*.

DISCUSSION

Expression of pheromone concentration in units gives a more accurate picture of the relative activity of the extracted insects and increases the size of the difference between allatectomized and control groups and between allatectomized and hormone-treated groups.

There is no significant difference either in pheromone activity or in egg maturation up to 10 days after emergence between normally fed females of *T. molitor* and those maintained on water only. Mordue (1967) has made similar observations on egg maturation in this species. In virgin females initial oöcyte development and pheromone secretion seem to be independent of food intake.

Removal of the entire head, the corpora cardiaca–allata, or the brain significantly reduces pheromone activity and causes total inhibition of egg maturation. The rôle of the corpora allata in the control of pheromone secretion has already been established in locusts (Loher, 1960) and in several species of cockroaches (Barth, 1961, 1962, 1965; Roth and Barth, 1964; Yamamoto cited in Barth, 1965). The results of allatectomy in *Tenebrio* are in agreement with these findings. Reimplantation of corpora allata into allatectomized insects was shown to restore pheromone secretion in locusts and cockroaches. However, in *Tenebrio* reimplantation of one pair of corpora allata had no effect. According to Mordue (1965), cutting the nervi corporis cardiaci I disrupts the proper functioning of the endocrine system in *Tenebrio* and impairs yolk deposition. He presented evidence suggesting that control of the corpora allata may be by way of axons other than those from intercerebral neurosecretory cells. Joly (1945) in *Dytiscus* and Staal (1961) in *Locusta* have shown that section of the nervi corporis allati impairs the secretory activity of the corpus allatum. A reciprocal relationship between corpora allata and the neurosecretory system has been demonstrated in *Periplaneta* (Nayar, 1962), *Calliphora* (Lea and Thomsen, 1962), *Schistocerca* (Highnam et al., 1963), and *Tenebrio* (Mordue, 1965). However, Laverdure (1967) has shown that implantation of active corpora allata from well-fed larvae is partially effective in inducing oöcyte maturation in allatectomized *Tenebrio* females. This suggests that the corpora allata require intact nervous connexion with the brain for active secretion but not for the release of their product. In the present experiments the implants (corpora allata) were taken from newly emerged adult females and were probably not active at the time of implantation, possibly accounting for their ineffectiveness in inducing pheromone secretion.

Removal of the brain also lowers pheromone level in *Tenebrio* females, indicating that the brain has some control over the process. Removal of the brain and corpora allata together, or decapitation, further lowers the pheromone activity, suggesting their synergistic relationship in stimulating pheromone production. However, reimplantation of brain into brainless females does not restore the pheromone level. It is possible that implantation of the entire cephalic complex would have been effective in restoring pheromone activity in deficient insects. According to LAVERDURE (1967) implantation of brain alone from well-fed larvae has some effect in inducing vitellogenesis in brainless unfed females, thereby indicating that neurosecretory cells of the brain of well-fed larvae can activate the corpora allata of unfed insects to some extent, even without a nervous connexion. The ineffectiveness of the brain implant from a newly-moulted adult may be due to a lack of stored neurosecretory product; deprived of its nervous connexions the capacity of the brain to synthesize neurohormone may have been impaired.

In order to determine if the corpus allatum hormone is important in controlling pheromone secretion, insects without corpora allata or head were treated with juvenile hormone analogues. This treatment was effective in restoring the pheromone activity of the experimentals to that of controls, thus indicating that the secretion of the corpora allata may be solely responsible for controlling pheromone activity. Brain and other centres do not seem to be directly involved in the process, although they seem to have a rôle in activating the corpora allata. BARTH and EMMERICH (1968) and EMMERICH and BARTH (1968) have shown that treatment with the juvenile hormone analogue, farnesyl methyl ether (one of the two analogues used herein on *Tenebrio*), promotes pheromone secretion in allatectomized *Byrsotria fumigata*.

All operations which lowered the pheromone activity also inhibited egg maturation in *Tenebrio*. Reimplantation of the brain or the corpora allata was also ineffective in inducing vitellogenesis, probably because the implants remained inactive. According to MORDUE (1965), a nervous connexion between the brain and corpora allata is essential for the occurrence of vitellogenesis in *Tenebrio*, whereas LAVERDURE (1967) has shown that the implanted larval brain or corpora allata are effective in inducing egg maturation in decerebrate or allatectomized *T. molitor*, respectively. Juvenile hormone analogues, in concentrations which restored pheromone activity in operated insects, apparently induced slight yolk deposition in allatectomized insects, but they were totally ineffective in inducing yolk deposition in decerebrate or decapitated insects. This may mean either that the hormone required for pheromone production is not sufficient for yolk deposition or that neurosecretory cells of the brain, in addition to regulating the corpora allata, exercise a direct control over oöcyte development. The brain in allatectomized insects may still induce the first growth phase of oöcytes, but juvenile hormone is needed for yolk deposition (*cf.* LAVERDURE, 1967). Although EMMERICH and BARTH (1968) found yolk deposition in allatectomized *B. fumigata* after treatment with farnesyl methyl ether, they considered pheromone production to be a more sensitive indicator of corpus allatum activity than oöcyte maturation, as the former is stimulated by a lower titre of corpus allatum hormone. CHEN *et al.* (1962) and BOWERS *et al.* (1965) have established the gonadotropic effect of juvenile hormone analogues in *Periplaneta*. JOLY (1965, 1969) has shown that juvenile hormone accelerates yolk deposition in *Locusta migratoria* and, according to BROZA and RICEVUTE (1969), juvenile hormone can break reproductive diapause in the grasshopper *Oedipoda miniata*. However, in all these cases the brain is still present to support the synthesis of protein which can be mobilized by juvenile hormone into yolk. WIGGLESWORTH (1963) has demonstrated yolk deposition by juvenile hormone in decapitated *Rhodnius*, and BROOKES (1969) in the isolated abdomens of *Leucophaea maderae*. However, no yolk deposition was observed with farnesol and farnesyl methyl ether in *Pyrrhocoris* (SLÁMA, 1965), and with cecropia oil in *Calliphora* (THOMSEN, 1959), in *Leptinotarsa* (DE WILDE, 1959), and in *Aedes* (WEIRCH, 1963).

Removal of the frontal ganglion did not significantly interfere with pheromone secretion, although it apparently had some inhibitory effect on egg maturation. CLARKE and LANGLEY (1961), CLARKE and GILLOT (1965), STRONG (1966), HIGHNAM *et al.* (1966), and HILL *et al.* (1966) have shown that the removal of the ganglion interfered with sexual maturation and ovarian development in locusts by disrupting the neurosecretory system. However, according to the above authors, ganglion-ectomy resulted in a more delayed effect than when corpora allata were removed. Since the present experiments on *Tenebrio* were terminated within 10 days of operation, there may not have been sufficient time for any considerable effect of removal of the frontal ganglion on pheromone production and egg maturation.

The fact that ovariectomy does not lower the pheromone activity in *Tenebrio* eliminates a rôle of the ovary in the control of pheromone secretion. The appearance of high pheromone activity coinciding with mature eggs in insects devoid of corpora allata may be due to some traces of juvenile hormone in the body (because of incomplete or late removal of the gland).

This study shows that there is an endocrine regulation of pheromone secretion in *T. molitor* and that the corpora allata are directly involved in the process. The rôle of the brain seems essential but indirect, an intact connexion between the brain and the corpora allata being necessary for the normal functioning of the latter.

Acknowledgements—Special thanks are due to my major professors, HOWARD A. BERN and RUDOLPH I. PIPA, for their valuable guidance and constructive criticisms throughout the course of this work and Professor RALPH I. SMITH for reading the manuscript. I am indebted to Mr. G. C. UNNITHAN for sharing the burden of biological assaying of the numerous extracts; to Dr. W. R. TSCHINKEL, Dr. J. NAISSE, and Dr. D. S. KING for constructive suggestions; and to Mr. S. BALASUBHRAMANIAN and Mr. W. C. CLARKE for advice on analysis of the data. I am thankful to Mrs. EMILY REID for making the diagrams; and Miss JOYCE BURNER, Mr. DAVID COHEN, and Mr. PETER SCHEAFFER for important assistance. Hoffman-LaRoche and Syntex-Zoëcon (Dr. JOHN SIDDALL) kindly supplied the juvenile hormone analogues. Aided by NSF grant GB-6424 to Professor BERN.

REFERENCES

AUGUST C. J. (1967) The pheromone mediation of the mating behavior of *Tenebrio molitor*. M.A. Thesis in Zoology, University of California, Los Angeles.

BARTH R. H., JR. (1961) Hormonal control of sex attractant production in the Cuban cockroach. *Science, Wash.* **133**, 1598–1599.

BARTH R. H., JR. (1962) The endocrine control of mating behavior in the cockroach *Byrsotria fumigata* (Guérin). *Gen. comp. Endocr.* **2**, 53–69.

BARTH R. H., JR. (1965) Insect mating behavior. Endocrine control of a chemical communication system. *Science, Wash.* **149**, 882.

BARTH R. H., JR. and EMMERICH, H. (1968) Effect of juvenile hormone analogues on the reproductive physiology of females of the cockroach, *Byrsotria fumigata* (Guérin). *Am. Zool.* **8**, 755.

BOWERS W. S., THOMPSON M. J., and UEBEL E. C. (1965) Juvenile and gonadotropic hormone activity of 10,11-epoxyfarnesinic acid methyl ester. *Life Sci.* **4**, 2323–2331.

BROOKES V. J. (1969) Maturation of the oöcytes in the isolated abdomen of *Leucophaea maderae*. *J. Insect Physiol.* **15**, 621–631.

BROZA M. and RICEVUTE C. (1969) Hormonal control of reproductive diapause in the grasshopper *Oedipoda miniata*. *Experientia* **25**, 414–415.

CHEN D. H., ROBBINS W. E., and MONROE R. E. (1962) The gonadotropic action of cecropia extract in allatectomized American cockroaches. *Experientia* **18**, 577–578.

CLARKE K. U. and GILLOT G. (1965) Relationship between the removal of the frontal ganglion and protein starvation in *Locusta migratoria* L. *Nature, Lond.* **208**, 808–809.

CLARKE K. U. and LANGLEY P. A. (1961) Effect of the removal of frontal ganglion on the development of the gonads in *Locusta migratoria* L. *Nature, Lond.* **198**, 811–812.

EMMERICH H. and BARTH R. H., JR. (1968) Effect of farnesyl methyl ether on reproductive physiology in the cockroach, *Byrsotria fumigata* (Guérin). *Z. Naturforsch.* **23b**, 1019–1020.

EPHRUSSI B. and BEADLE G. W. (1936) A technique of transplantation for *Drosophila*. *Am. Nat.* **70**, 218–225.

HAPP G. M. (1969) Multiple sex pheromones of the mealworm beetle *Tenebrio molitor*. *Nature, Lond.* **222**, 180–181.

HIGHNAM K. C., HILL L., and MORDUE W. (1966) The endocrine system and oöcyte growth in *Schistocerca* in relation to starvation and frontal ganglionectomy. *J. Insect Physiol.* **12**, 977–994.

HIGHNAM K. C., LUSIS O., and HILL L. (1963) The rôle of corpora allata during oöcyte growth in the desert locust, *Schistocerca gregaria* Forsk. *J. Insect Physiol.* **9**, 587–596.

HILL L., MORDUE W., and HIGHNAM K. C. (1966) Endocrine system, frontal ganglion, and feeding during maturation in the female desert locust. *J. Insect Physiol.* **12**, 1197–1208.

JOLY P. (1945) La fonction ovarienne et son contrôle humoral chez les Dytiscidés. *Arch. Zool. exp. gén.* **84**, 49–164.

JOLY P. (1965) Réactions de *Locusta migratoria* aux substances juvénilisantes. *Gen. comp. Endocr.* **5**, 689–690.

JOLY P. (1969) Résultats d'injections de fortes doses d'hormone juvénile à *Locusta migratoria* en phase grégaire. *C.R. Acad. Sci., Paris* **268**, 1634–1635.

LAVERDURE A. M. (1967) Rôles de l'alimentation et des hormones cérébrales dans la vitellogenèse chez *Tenebrio molitor* (Coléoptère). *Bull. Soc. zool. Fr.* **92**, 629–640.

LEA A. O. and THOMSEN E. (1962) Cycles in the synthetic activity of the medial neurosecretory cells of *Calliphora erythrocephala* and their regulation. *Mem. Soc. Endocr.* **12**, 345–347.

LOHER W. (1960) The chemical acceleration of maturation process and its hormonal control in the desert locust. *Proc. R. Soc.* (B) **153**, 380–397.

MORDUE W. (1965) Neuro-endocrine factors in the control of oöcyte production in *Tenebrio molitor* L. *J. Insect Physiol.* **11**, 617–629.

MORDUE W. (1967) The influence of feeding upon the activity of the neuroendocrine system during oöcyte growth in *Tenebrio molitor*. *Gen. comp. Endocr.* **9**, 406–415.

146

NAYAR K. K. (1962) Effects of injecting juvenile hormone extracts on the neurosecretory system of adult male cockroaches (*Periplaneta americana*). *Mem. Soc. Endocr.* **12**, 371–378.

NORRIS M. J. and PENER M. P. (1965) An inhibitory effect of allatectomized males and females on the sexual maturation of young male adults of *Schistocerca gregaria* Forsk. (Orthoptera: Acrididae) *Nature, Lond.* **208**, 1122.

ROTH L. M. and BARTH R. H. JR. (1964) Control of sexual receptivity in female cockroaches. *J. Insect Physiol.* **10**, 965–975.

SLÁMA K. (1965) The effect of hormone mimetic substances on the ovarian development and oxygen consumption in allatectomized adult females of *Pyrrhocoris apterus* L. (Hemiptera). *J. Insect Physiol.* **11**, 1121–1129.

STAAL G. B. JR. (1961) Studies on the physiology of phase induction in *Locusta migratoria migratorioides* R. et F. Thesis, Wageningen, Holland, pp. 125—Also in: *Pub. Fonds Landb. Expert Bur.* p. 40.

STEEL R. G. D. and TORRIE J. H. (1960) *Principles and Procedures of Statistics.* McGraw-Hill, New York.

STRONG L. (1966) Effect of removal of the frontal ganglion on corpus allatum function in *Locusta migratoria migratorioides* R. and F. *Nature, Lond.* **210**, 330–331.

THOMSEN E. (1959) (In panel discussion.) *Acta Symp. Evol. Ins., Prague,* p. 218.

TSCHINKEL W. R., WILLSON C., and BERN H. A. (1967) Sex pheromone of the mealworm beetle *Tenebrio molitor* L. *J. exp. Zool.* **164**, 81–86.

VALENTINE J. M. (1931) The olfactory sense of the adult mealworm beetle *Tenebrio molitor* L. *J. exp. Zool.* **58**, 165–227.

WEIRCH G. (1963) Zur Frage der hormonalen Regulation der Eireifung bei Insekten. Inaug. Dissert. Naturwiss. Fak. Ludwig-Masimillians Universität, München.

WIGGLESWORTH V. B. (1963) Juvenile hormone effect of farnesol and some related compounds: Quantitative experiments. *J. Insect Physiol.* **9**, 105–119.

DE WILDE J. (1959) (In panel discussion.) *Acta Symp. Evol. Ins., Prague,* p. 219.

ZDAREK J. (1968) Le comportement d'accouplement à la fin de la diapause imaginale et contrôle hormonal dans le cas de la punaise *Pyrrhocoris apterus* L. (Pyrrhocoridae, Heteroptera). *Ann. Endocr. Paris* **29**, 703–707.

Sex Pheromones of Noctuid Moths. XXI. Light:Dark Cycle Regulation and Light Inhibition of Sex Pheromone Release by Females of *Trichoplusia ni*[1,2]

L. L. SOWER, H. H. SHOREY, and LYLE K. GASTON

ABSTRACT

Females of *Trichoplusia ni* (Hübner) synchronized to a 12:12 light:dark cycle at 24°C released sex pheromone only between 5 hours after dark and the end of the dark period. Peak release occurred from 8 to 11 hours after dark. The time of mating appears to be regulated by an endogenous circadian rhythm of female pheromone release. The numbers of females releasing pheromone per night were inversely correlated to light intensities of between 0.3 and 300 lux.

Regulation of mating activity of noctuid moths is affected by a number of environmental factors. Mating between caged males and females of *Trichoplusia ni* (Hübner), the cabbage looper moth, is inhibited by light intensities greater than 0.3 lux (Shorey 1966). Also, male responsiveness to the female sex pheromone was found to decrease at light intensities above 0.3 lux (Shorey and Gaston 1964). However, this correlation does not necessarily indicate that the inhibition of mating is caused entirely by reduced male responsiveness; it may be attributed also to a reduction in the tendency of females to release pheromone.

In laboratory colonies of *T. ni* a circadian rhythm of male responsiveness to the female sex pheromone

[1] Lepidoptera: Noctuidae.
[2] This investigation was supported in part by Public Health Service Grant no. GM 11524–06 from the National Institute of General Medical Sciences, U. S. Public Health Service. Received for publication Oct. 20, 1969.

occurs, with peak responses between 6 and 7 hr after the beginning of a 12-hr dark period (Shorey and Gaston 1965). This is similar to a curve depicting the time of mating, that peaks between 8 and 9 hr after dark (Shorey 1966). However, evidence has been given (Callahan 1958, Shorey 1964, Shorey and Gaston 1965) that the time of mating among noctuid moths is controlled by the female, through her release of sex pheromone.

The release of sex pheromone by *T. ni* females is characterized by a dorsoposterior extension of the abdomen accompanied by elevation, and often vibration, of the wings. The sex pheromone gland, situated between abdominal segments 8 and 9 (Jefferson et al. 1966), is visibly exposed to the air. Females in the laboratory normally remain stationary while releasing pheromone and cling to the sides or the top interior surface of their cage. It has been stated (Shorey 1964) that males attempted copulation only with females which were engaged in this characteristic behavior.

The research reported here was concerned with determining the influence of various light cycles and intensities on the timing and occurrence of pheromone release by *T. ni* females.

METHODS AND MATERIALS

The moths were reared using previously reported methods (Shorey and Hale 1965). Environmental conditions, from the pupal stage on, were $24\pm2°C$ at a 12:12 light:dark cycle (light intensity equaled ca. 350 lux). The insects were held in $30\times30\times30$ cm screen cages and fed 8% sucrose solution. All females used for observation were 3–8 days old.

Fig. 1 shows a schematic diagram of the apparatus used for observation of females. It consisted of an elongated wooden box painted flat black inside, with the top closed with a heavy black cloth. The observation chamber at 1 end was also hooded with black cloth, allowing access to the observer without admission of room light. Light intensities of 0.3, 3, and 30 lux were obtained by displacing a 7.5-w incandescent bulb appropriate distances from the observation chamber. For 300 lux, a 100-w bulb was substituted. Blower ventilation of the light bulb holding chamber was required at 300 lux to prevent excessive heating. Qualitative spectral differences between the 2 bulbs were minimal, relative to quantitative differences, when measured with an ISCO model SR spectroradiometer at wavelengths of 5000–11,000 A. One thickness of Accuracy, 50% cotton fiber, 20 lb bond typing paper, formed a fairly uniform backlighted

149

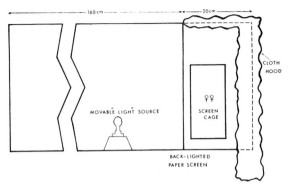

FIG. 1.—Schematic diagram of the apparatus used to observe sex pheromone releasing behavior of *T. ni* females.

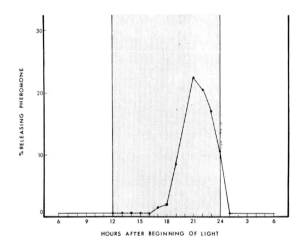

FIG. 2.—The circadian rhythm of sex pheromone release by females of *T. ni* entrained to a 12:12 light:dark cycle at 24°C. The shaded area represents darkness.

surface between the light source and the observation chamber. Light intensities in the observation chamber were measured with a Photovolt no. 200C photometer; the probe was held 1 cm from the center of the lighted paper surface.

To determine pheromone release patterns, females were held in cylindrical 11-cm-diam × 21-cm copper-screen cages placed 1 cm from the lighted surface in the observation chamber. The specific criterion used to recognize a releasing female was distinct visibility of the pheromone gland or the extended terminal abdominal segments. The nightly rhythm of pheromone release (Fig. 2) was determined by observation of females at 1-hr intervals throughout the dark period at 0.3 lux (19 replications of 5–10 ♀ each, n = 180).

The pheromone-release rhythm was further investigated by observation of females through continu-

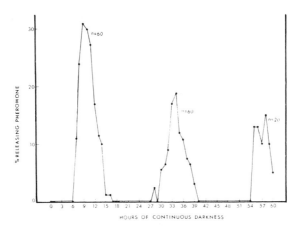

FIG. 3.—Sex pheromone release curves of *T. ni* females entrained to a 12:12 light:dark cycle and observed through an extended dark period.

ous dark periods (0.3 lux) for 36–60 hr beginning at the start of a normal dark period (Fig. 3); with these females, sucrose solution was made available at all times. Observations were made at 0.5- to 1-hr intervals throughout the extended dark period.

For light-inhibition tests, 10 ♀ were placed in each of 2 cages in the observation chamber 5 hr after the start of darkness and observed at 30-min intervals beginning at the 6th hr. Six replicates of 20 ♀ at each of 4 light intensities (0.3, 3, 30, 300 lux) were completed. Locomotory activity, any movement by females not releasing pheromone, was also recorded. Fig. 4 summarizes the results.

RESULTS AND DISCUSSION

Pheromone release behavior occurred between 5 hr after the onset of a 12-hr dark period and the beginning of the light period (Fig. 2). Peak release occurred between 8 and 11 hr after dark. This nightly rhythm corresponds closely to a mating curve determined under similar environmental conditions (Shorey 1966). It appears probable that the mating curve is determined by the female rhythm of calling rather than by male activity. The corresponding nightly rhythm of male responsiveness to 10^{-3} female equivalent of sex pheromone on filter paper (Shorey and Gaston 1965) is much broader, encompassing the entire dark period. Significantly, this male curve peaks just prior to the time of maximum female pheromone release. We assume that mating, in confined laboratory cages, occurs very shortly after a female begins releasing sex pheromone. As one would expect, male and female sexual activity cycles are not independent.

Part of the data forming Fig. 2 were gathered from females (n = 60) under a 12:12 light:dark cycle 5 hr out of synchronization from the rest of the observed females (n = 120). That the 2 sets of data were homogeneous is evidence for entrainment of the pheromone-release rhythm simply by the light:dark cycle. Whether temperature variations or other environmental changes will modify this rhythm has not

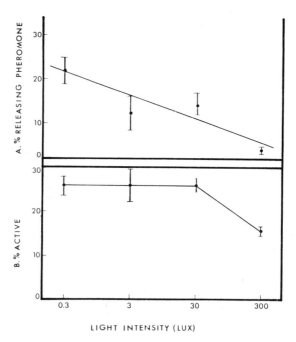

LIGHT INTENSITY (LUX)

Fig. 4.—Average percentages of *T. ni* females engaged in sex pheromone releasing behavior (A) or in locomotory activity (B) between 7 and 12 hr after the onset of darkness at 4 light intensities. Vertical lines indicate standard errors. The correlation coefficient (r = 0.91) for part A is significant at the 0.05 probability level.

yet been determined in the laboratory. However it was found previously (Shorey 1966) that a mating curve of caged moths held in the varying conditions of the field did not synchronize with the laboratory mating curve.

Fairly consistent maintenance of the pheromone-release cycle (Fig. 3) is evident for periods of up to 60 hr of continuous darkness (actually, a constant low light intensity of 0.3 lux). This endogeneity is further evidence indicating a true circadian rhythm which is entrained by the light:dark cycle. Decreasing magnitudes of pheromone release during the 2nd and 3rd sexual activity cycles of the extended dark period (Fig. 3) are at least partially due to loss of vigor, including deaths, among the observed females.

Females observed during the 1st activity cycle of the extended dark period *gradually* reduced their sex pheromone release frequencies after passing the 12th hr, when the light normally would have come on (Fig. 3). In contrast, Fig. 2 shows an *abrupt cessation* of pheromone release immediately after the beginning of the light period, indicating some light-inhibition affect.

Increasing light intensities from 0.3 to 300 lux, during the normal dark period, progressively inhibited pheromone release (Fig. 4A). Locomotory activity levels were not inhibited until the light intensity was raised to the maximum of 300 lux (Fig. 4B). Therefore, progressive light inhibition of mating (Shorey 1966) is correlated with both light inhibition of pheromone release by the females and with inhibition of pheromone responsiveness by the males (Shorey and Gaston 1964).

REFERENCES CITED

Callahan, P. S. 1958. Behavior of the imago of the corn earworm, *Heliothis zea* (Boddie), with special reference to emergence and reproduction. Ann. Entomol. Soc. Amer. 51 : 271–83.

Jefferson, R. N., H. H. Shorey, and L. K. Gaston. 1966. Sex pheromones of noctuid moths. X. The morphology and histology of the female sex pheromone gland of *Trichoplusia ni* (Lepidoptera: Noctuidae). Ibid. 59 : 1166–9.

Shorey, H. H. 1964. Sex pheromones of noctuid moths. II. Mating behavior of *Trichoplusia ni* (Lepidoptera: Noctuidae) with special reference to the role of the sex pheromone. Ibid. 57 : 371–7.

1966. The biology of *Trichoplusia ni* (Lepidoptera: Noctuidae). IV. Environmental control of mating. Ibid. 59 : 502–6.

Shorey, H. H., and L. K. Gaston. 1964. Sex pheromones of noctuid moths. III. Inhibition of male responses to the sex pheromone in *Trichoplusia ni* (Lepidoptera: Noctuidae). Ibid. 57 : 775–9.

1965. Sex pheromones of noctuid moths. V. Circadian rhythm of pheromone responsiveness in males of *Autographa californica, Heliothis virescens, Spodop-*

tera exigua, and *Trichoplusia   ni* (Lepidoptera: Noctuidae). Ibid. 58: 597–600.

Shorey, H. H., and R. L. Hale. 1965. Mass rearing of the larvae of nine noctuid species on a simple artificial medium. J. Econ. Entomol. 58: 522–4.

ROLE OF THE CORPORA CARDIACA IN THE BEHAVIOR OF SATURNIID MOTHS. I. RELEASE OF SEX PHEROMONE

LYNN M. RIDDIFORD AND CARROLL M. WILLIAMS

Mating of Polyphemus moths under laboratory conditions requires the presence of a volatile emanation from oak leaves (Riddiford and Williams, 1967). The active material has been extracted from red oak leaves and shown to be *trans*-2-hexenal (Riddiford, 1967). Vapors of a dilute solution of this aldehyde were found to act upon the female antennae. The resulting nervous input to the brain provokes after a certain period of delay the "calling" behavior. The latter can be recognized by inspection in terms of the protrusion of the female genitalia thereby exposing the glands which emit the sex pheromone.

In the case of virgin Cercropia females, calling behavior is elicited, not by a chemical, but by photoperiod. Thus, under both long- and short-day conditions, calling begins 1.5 to 2 hours before dawn and often continues for as long as 0.5 hour after lights-on. During this same pre-dawn period, male Cecropia moths become hyperactive even in the absence of females.

The third silkmoth considered in the present study was *Antheraea pernyi*—a semi-domesticated species which, like the completely domesticated *Bombyx mori,* has for thousands of years been selected for ease of mating. Though virgin Pernyi females show no overt calling behavior under laboratory conditions, there is convincing evidence that the sex pheromone is continuously released to provoke mating at any time of day or night (Riddiford, 1970).

In the present study carried out on these three species we have sought to determine whether the corpora cardiaca or corpora allata are involved in the control of the release of sex pheromone.

MATERIALS AND METHODS

1. *Experimental animals*

Pupae of *Antheraea polyphemus* and *Hyalophora cecropia* were purchased from dealers or reared outdoors on netted trees (Telfer, 1967). Cocoons of *Antheraea pernyi* were obtained from Japanese sources. The pupae were stored at 5° C for at least 12 weeks; they were then returned to 25° C to provoke adult development.

2. *Excision of corpora allata and/or corpora cardiaca*

These organs were removed from pupae by the technique described by Williams (1959). To check the completeness of extirpation, the excised organs were placed in a black dish containing Ringer's solution and examined under a dissecting microscope. If the excised organs were not self-evident, the extirpation was considered incomplete and the animal was discarded. In certain individuals the glandular complexes were excised and three pairs of "loose" complexes reimplanted into the thoracic tergum. All individuals were placed at 25° C under controlled photoperiod (usually 17L:7D). Adult development was initiated after about 2 weeks and completed after an additional 3 weeks.

3. *Behavioral assays*

Female Polyphemus moths were caged in a darkened room and exposed to the vapors of 0.05% aqueous *trans*-2-hexenal solution. The experiment was usually begun in the early evening. At half-hour intervals for at least the first 4 hours, the moths were inspected under dim red light for calling behavior; they were again inspected the following morning.

In the experiments performed on Cecropia the female moths were reared and caged in two constant-temperature rooms, one programmed for a short day (12L:12D) and the other for a long day (17L:7D). Under dim red light the moths were inspected for calling behavior at hourly intervals throughout the scotophase.

In the experiments performed on *A. pernyi,* virgin females were caged with males and their mating behavior ascertained as described by Riddiford (1970).

EXPERIMENTAL RESULTS

1. *Delay in response of virgin female Polyphemus moths to vapors of trans-2-hexenal*

As described under Methods, 46 normal females were caged in a darkened room in the presence of the vapors of *trans*-2-hexenal. Observations under dim red light at 0.5 hour intervals indicated that at least one hour was required for the initiation of calling behavior and that 74% of individuals were calling after a total of 4 hours.

More detailed observations were carried out on a series of 9 virgin females which were placed, 1 or 2 at a time, in a 2-liter glass chamber in a darkened room. The chamber was ventilated by a gentle stream of air containing the vapors of a 0.05% aqueous solution of *trans*-2-hexenal. Observations of the moths were made at 15-minute intervals under dim red light.

The results summarized in Figure 1 once again show that at least an hour elapses before the first individual initiates calling. Fifty per cent of individuals initiated calling within the first 2.25 hours and 100% within the first 4 hours. From these observations we learn that a latent. period intervenes between the

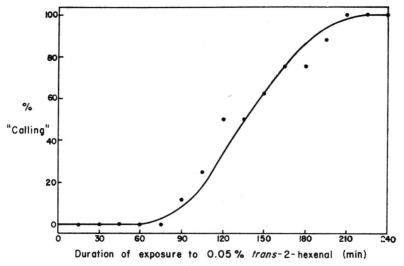

FIGURE 1. The time required for virgin Polyphemus females to begin releasing sex pheromone ("calling") after exposure to vapors of an aqueous solution of 0.05% *trans-2-* hexenal in the apparatus described under Materials and Methods. A total of 9 moths was used in these determinations.

presentation of the chemical stimulus and the initiation of the behavioral response. This delay was the first indication that a neuroendocrine relay mechanism might be involved.

2. Effects of allatectomy

The corpora allata were excised from 20 female Polyphemus pupae without any damage to the nearby copora cardiaca. The allatectomized pupae were then placed at 25° C and allowed to develop into adult moths. The latter's response to *trans-2-*hexenal was then determined as described under Methods. The results summarized in Figure 2 are the same as seen for unoperated Polyphemus moths. Moreover, the allatectomized females mated when placed with males and oviposited a normal number of eggs which hatched as normal first-instar larvae.

The experiment was repeated on 19 allatectomized Cecropia moths exposed to the short-day regimen of 12L:12D. Normal behavior was observed in terms of the presence of calling behavior during the final hour before lights-on. The results summarized in Figure 2 show that the absence of corpora allata in no way affected the response to photoperiod.

3. Effects of removal of the complex of corpora cardiaca and corpora allata

The experiment described in the preceding section was repeated on 29 Polyphemus and 38 Cecropia except that in this case the moths were derived from pupae lacking the entire complex of corpora allata and corpora cardiaca. The results summarized in Figure 2 show a great departure from normal behavior in that fewer than 20% of individuals showed calling behavior in response to the appropriate stimuli.

At the conclusion of the experiment many of the moths, including all individuals which had shown a calling response, were sacrificed. The heads were excised, pinned under Ringer's solution, and carefully inspected for any trace of the excised glands. The several individuals which showed any such indications were eliminated from the experiment. In Figure 2 the 14 to 18% of individuals which displayed

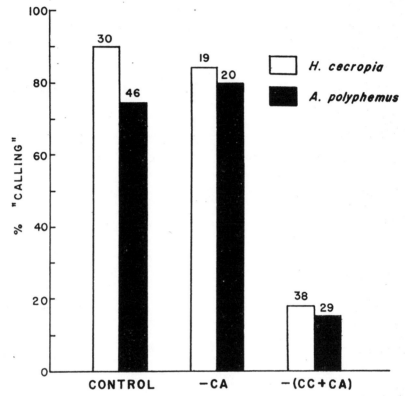

FIGURE 2. The effect of allatectomy and allatectomy-cardiactomy on the "calling" response of Polyphemus and Cecropia females to vapors of 0.05% *trans*-2-hexenal and to photoperiod respectively. The numbers in parentheses above the bars indicate the number of females tested.

the calling response showed no trace of corpora cardiaca. However, the dissection is a difficult one so there remains the possibility that the extirpation may have been incomplete in these individuals.

4. *Re-implantation of the corpora allata-corpora cardiaca complexes*

The glandular complexes were excised from 11 female Polyphemus pupae and 2 female Cecropia pupae. Into the thoracic tergum of each individual were immediately reimplanted 3 pairs of "loose" glandular complexes. The moths derived from these preparations were tested for calling in response to the appropriate stimuli. The results were as follows: only 2 (18%) of the Polyphemus moths showed calling behavior when exposed to *trans*-2-hexenal vapors; none of the Cecropia moths showed calling behavior in response to photoperiod.

5. *Effects of denervating the corpora cardiaca*

In 5 female Polyphemus pupae the two pairs of nerves connecting the corpora cardiaca with the rear of the brain were severed. When the moths derived from these preparations were challenged with vapors of *trans*-2-hexenal, they showed no trace of the normal calling response. At the conclusion of the experiment autopsies performed on all 5 individuals showed no regeneration of the connections between brain and corpora cardiaca.

6. *Experiment on female Pernyi moths*

As mentioned in the introduction, *Antheraea pernyi* is a semi-domesticated species which has been highly selected for ease of mating. In experiments reported by Barth (1965) the allatectomized female Pernyi moths were fully effective in attracting and mating with males. The question therefore arises as to whether they can do so if the corpora cardiaca are also extirpated. To answer this question we excised the complex of corpora allata and corpora cardiaca from 16 female Pernyi pupae. The moths derived from these individuals were tested for the release of sex pheromone by caging them with normal males. Fifteen of the 16 females mated within 15 minutes, thereby documenting the continuous release of sex pheromone peculiar to the virgin females of this species.

DISCUSSION

1. *The role of the corpora cardiaca in the reproductive behavior of virgin female silkmoths*

In contrast to the continous and apparently spontaneous release of sex pheromone by virgin females of semi-domesticated Pernyi silkmoths, the undomesticated Cecropia and Polyphemus silkmoths possess a neuro-endocrine mechanism for the control of pheromone release. Our experiments strongly argue that the corpora cardiaca, but not the corpora allata, are necessary for the calling behavior which accompanies the release of sex pheromone by the virgin female moths. That being so, the excision of the corpora cardiaca blocks the normal release of pheromone in response to environmental signals. This loss is not repaired by the reimplantation of as many as three pairs of "loose" glandular complexes—a finding which suggests that the nervous connections between the brain and corpora cardiaca are necessary for the behavioral response. When these nervous connections were selectively severed, calling behavior was blocked despite the continued presence of the denervated corpora cardiaca.

Females lacking corpora cardiaca fail to mate because males are not attracted to them. However, when caged with males near a cage of normal calling females, they not only mate, but then go on to lay fertile eggs. The absence of corpora

159

cardiaca therefore interferes with the attraction of males but not with the ability to mate and reproduce.

2. Dual role of the corpora cardiaca

The corpora cardiaca serve as neurohaemal organs in which the products of the brain's neurosecretory cells are released into the blood. In addition, the corpora cardiaca contain intrinsic neurosecretory cells and therefore qualify as genuine endocrine organs. When the corpora cardiaca are excised, their intrinsic cells are permanently lost, whereas the neurohaemal portion promptly regenerates from the cut ends of *nervi corpora cardiaci* I and II (Stumm-Zollinger, 1957). So, for our present purposes it appears that the intrinsic cells of the corpora cardiaca are the source of the hormone which triggers the calling behavior of virgin females.

3. The minimal circuitry

In virgin Cecropia and Polyphemus moths the brain processes in-coming signals conveying specific environmental cues relating to the onset and timing of reproductive behavior. After this central integration, signals flow from the brain to the corpora cardiaca via the two pairs of nerves which interconnect them. On the basis of present knowledge we cannot say whether these signals are nerve impulses or neurosecretory agents. The signals in question converge on the intrinsic cells of the corpora cardiaca to provoke the release from these cells of a certain hormone. In the case of cockroaches, Milburn and Roeder (1962) have extracted from the corpora cardiaca a substance which causes rhythmic discharge in the phallic nerve when applied to the abdominal ganglia. Evidently, in the virgin moths an analogous factor is secreted by the intrinsic cells of the corpora cardiaca to promote the motor acts which comprise the calling behavior.

A similar type of mechanism involved in oviposition behavior will be examined in the further detail in the following communication (Truman and Riddiford, 1971).

Supported by NSF grants GB-7966 (LMR) and GB-7963 (CMW) and by the Rockefeller Foundation. We wish to thank Dr. James Truman for preparation of the figures and for a critical reading of the manuscript.

SUMMARY

1. In virgin female silkmoths the protrusion of the genitalia or "calling" behavior signals sex pheromone release. The wild Polyphemus and Cecropia silkmoths "call" in response to specific environmental cues which are chemical and photoperiodic respectively. The semi-domesticated Pernyi silkmoth is exceptional in that it shows no overt "calling" behavior and pheromone is apparently released continuously.

2. By appropriate experiments it was possible to show that the corpora cardiaca but not the corpora allata are prerequisite for the "calling" behavior. Thus, when the corpora allata are removed from female pupae, the behavior of the resulting

160

moths is normal. By contrast, removal of the corpora allata-corpora cardiaca complex greatly reduces the number which "call."

3. In order to perform their function in the "calling" behavior the corpora cardiaca must have intact connections with the brain. Reimplantation of three pairs of corpora allata-corpora cardiaca complexes into animals lacking their own complexes fails to restore the ability to "call." "Calling" is also blocked when the nervous connections between the corpora cardiaca and the brain are severed.

4. Evidently, in response to the environmental signals the brain stimulates the release of a hormone from the intrinsic cells of the corpora cardiaca. This hormone then acts on the abdominal nervous system to provoke the protrusion of the female genitalia and the accompanying release of pheromone.

LITERATURE CITED

BARTH, R. H., JR., 1965. Insect mating behaviour: endocrine control of a chemical communication system. *Science*, **149**: 882–883.

MILBURN, N., AND K. D. ROEDER, 1962. Control of efferent activity in the cockroach terminal abdominal ganglion by extracts of corpora cardiaca. *J. Gen. Comp. Physiol.*, **2**: 70–76.

RIDDIFORD, L. M., 1967. *Trans*-2-hexenal: mating stimulant for Polyphemus moths. *Science*, **158**: 139–141.

RIDDIFORD, L. M., 1970. Antennal proteins of saturniid moths: their possible role in olfaction. *J. Insect Physiol.*, **16**: 653–660.

RIDDIFORD, L. M., AND C. M. WILLIAMS, 1967. Volatile principle from oak leaves: role in sex life of the Polyphemus moth. *Science*, **155**: 589–590.

STUMM-ZOLLINGER, E., 1957. Histological study of regenerative processes after transection of the nervi corporis cardiaci in transplanted brains of the Cecropia silkworm (*Platysamia cecropia* L.). *J. Exp. Zool.*, **134**: 315–326.

TELFER, W., 1967. Cecropia. Pages 173–182 in F. H. Wilt and N. K. Wessells, Eds., *Methods in Developmental Biology*. Thomas Y. Crowell Co., New York.

TRUMAN, J. W., AND L. M. RIDDIFORD, 1971. Role of the corpora cardiaca in the behavior of saturniid moths. II. Oviposition. *Biol. Bull.*, **140**: 8–14.

WILLIAMS, C. M., 1959. The juvenile hormone. I. Endocrine activity of the corpora allata of the adult Cecropia silkworm. *Biol. Bull.*, **116**: 323–338.

Production of Aggregating Pheromones in Re-Emerged Parent Females of the Southern Pine Beetle[1,2]

JACK E. COSTER[3]

Investigations of bark beetle pheromones have been concerned largely with the occurrence of these chemicals in virgin beetles. In many Scolytidae, the parent adults re-emerge from an initially attacked host tree after they have completed egg-gallery construction and oviposition in the tree. These parent adults may attack another tree and establish another brood. Very little is known about pheromone production and field attractiveness of such beetles.

The aggregating pheromone of the southern pine beetle, *Dendroctonus frontalis* Zimmerman, has been identified as a mixture of 2 compounds, the terpene alcohol *trans*-verbenol and a unique bicyclic compound known as frontalin (Kinzer et al. 1969). These substances are contained in the hindgut of emergent females and are released to the outside where, along with host odors, they bring about aggregation of both sexes at trees undergoing attack (Vité and Renwick 1968). The pheromone content of female hindguts declines rapidly as feeding and gallery construction progress (Coster 1970[4]).

PROCEDURES

Source of Beetles.—Re-emerged southern pine beetles were obtained from trees that had been mass attacked. Logs cut from such trees were placed in outdoor rearing cages and the parent beetles were collected from the cages daily. Re-emergence of parent adults began 10–15 days after the tree was mass-attacked. Virgin adults were collected in the same way as they matured and emerged from naturally attacked pine logs. Beetles were sexed according to the presence of the transverse pronotal ridge in the females (Osgood and Clark 1963).

Field Bioassay.—Beetles were introduced into loblolly pine posts (13 cm $\times$ 2.3 m) for field bioassay in the fol-

[1] Coleoptera: Scolytidae.
[2] A portion of a dissertation accepted by the Graduate College of the Texas A&M University in partial fulfillment of the requirements for the Ph.D. degree. The work was supported by the Southern Forest Research Institute, Houston, Tex. Approved for publication as TA 8266 by the Director, Texas Agricultural Experiment Station. Received for publication Jan. 30, 1970.
[3] Present address: East Texas Research and Extension Center, Texas A&M University, Overton 75684.
[4] J. E. Coster. 1970. Certain aspects of pheromone release and aggregation behavior in the southern pine beetle. (Coleoptera: Scolytidae). Ph.D. dissertation, Texas A&M University. 129 p.

lowing way: a blunted 10-penny nail was driven through the pine bark to the cambium. One live female beetle was placed in each hole, and the hole was covered with a small square of plastic screen that was firmly stapled to the bark. Ten posts were prepared. Five contained 100 re-emerged females and each of the remaining contained 100 virgin females.

Bioassay of the posts was performed at forest sites adjacent to infestations of the beetles. The posts were concurrently bioassayed using tree-trunk-simulating olfactometers (Vité and Renwick 1968) modified to allow insertion of a pine post. The olfactometers consisted of a 28-cm × 2.5-m canvas sleeve fastened to a cylinder base. The sleeve was kept inflated by the air flow from an electric blower.

GLC Analysis.—Hindguts of female southern pine beetles were analyzed using gas-liquid chromatography (GLC). Frontalin and *trans*-verbenol were detected using a Varian 1200 chromatograph equipped with a flame ionization detector and a Varian A-20 recorder. The column was ⅛-in. × 5-ft stainless steel with 3% SE-30 on 100/120-mesh Varaport 30. Nitrogen and hydrogen flow rates were 25 ml/min. The column temperature was programmed from an initial temperature of 70°C to a final temperature of 140°C at a rate of 4°/min. Injector and detector temperatures were both held at 190°C. Synthetic frontalin and *trans*-verbenol were obtained from the Battelle Memorial Institute, Columbus, Ohio, for GLC verification purposes.

Six samples of re-emerged female hindguts were analyzed. Each sample consisted of 10 hindguts in 20 µliter of hexane. The solution was ground with a small amount of purified sand and then centrifuged. One µliter of each extract was subjected to GLC analysis. A sample of virgin females was prepared and analyzed in the same way.

RESULTS AND DISCUSSION

Field Bioassay.—In the field tests, live feeding virgin female southern pine beetles were 4.5 times more attractive than live feeding re-emerged females (Table 1). The total number of successful attacks by the introduced virgin females was 177. Re-emerged females made 119 successful attacks. This difference in number of attacks was significant (χ^2=11.4, 1 df), indicating perhaps less attack vigor by the re-emerged females. Evaluation of the response data of Table 1 in terms of successful attacks for each of the 2 beetle classes reveals that virgin beetles attracted 3.02 times as many beetles from the flying population as the re-emerged beetles. The sex ratio of the responding beetles was arrayed into a 2×2 contingency table and tested for independence. The ratio of sexes at the 2 classes of females did not vary significantly from each other (adjusted χ^2=1.29, 1 df).

GLC Analysis.—From the GLC studies, the mean peak areas (mm²) and the standard deviation for the 2 compounds from the 6 re-emerged female samples were: frontalin 25±24.9; *trans*-verbenol 996±491.4. The peak areas for the virgin hindguts were: frontalin 103; *trans-*

163

Table 1.—Field response of *D. frontalis* at olfactometers baited with loblolly pine posts containing 100 re-emerged parent females or 100 virgin females each.

| | No. beetles trapped | | |
| | Condition of feeding females | | |
Trial no.	Re-emerged	Virgin	Total
1	21	47	68
2	7	45	52
3	7	21	28
4	6	3	9
5	1	72	73
Total	42	188	230
Sex ratio of responding beetles (males : females)	26 : 12	100 : 76	

verbenol 1920 mm^2. Virgin female southern pine beetles contained 4.1 times as much frontalin and 1.9 times as much *trans*-verbenol as the re-emerged beetles. This fact substantiates the field-response data where virgin females attracted about 4.5 times as many beetles as the re-emerged females.

It is clear from these results that mating does not irreversibly inhibit pheromone production in female southern pine beetles. Although the pheromone content of the females declines to a low level during gallery construction (Coster 1970[4]), the females again are capable of producing significant attraction upon re-emergence.

Furthermore, the occurrence of the pheromones in re-emerged females points out the inappropriateness of designating these chemical messengers solely as "sex pheromones." A 2nd mating is not required by re-emerged southern pine beetle females for them to lay viable eggs (Yu and Tsao 1967). Therefore, production of a "sex" pheromone by such females would appear to be superfluous. Aggregation has high survival value for the southern pine beetle in that a host tree must be mass attacked for its oleoresin resistance mechanism to be overcome (Thatcher 1960, Vité and Pitman 1968). Failure of the beetles to attack a tree en masse may result in decimation of the beetle population, so the evolutionary value of the pheromone as an aggregant is at least as important as its value as a mating facilitant. Sexual behavior in the aggregations may have been a secondary development resulting from the greatly increased number of sexual encounters in the aggregations (Haskell 1966).

Re-emerging parent adults are an important and often overlooked consideration in southern pine beetle investigations. In the present study, 50–60% of the attacking population re-emerged in the laboratory rearing cages. These beetles form a significant portion of natural populations and may account for some of the variations in response and pheromone-producing abilities of southern pine beetles obtained from wild populations.

ACKNOWLEDGMENT

I thank Dr. J. P. Vité, Director of the Boyce Thompson Institute's Beaumont, Texas laboratory, for his help with the research and for the use of facilities and equipment.

REFERENCES CITED

Haskell, P. T. 1966. Flight behavior. *In* P. T. Haskell [ed.] Insect Behavior. Symp. Roy. Entomol. Soc. London (1965).

Kinzer, G. W., A. F. Fentiman, Jr., T. F. Page, Jr., R. L. Foltz, J. P. Vité, and G. B. Pitman. 1969. Bark beetle attractants: Identification, synthesis, and field bioassay of a new compound isolated from *Dendroctonus.* Nature 221: 477–8.

Osgood, E. A., and E. W. Clark. 1963. Methods of sexing and sex ratios of the southern pine beetle *Dendroctonus frontalis* Zimm. Can. Entomol. 95: 1106–9.

Thatcher, R. G. 1960. Bark beetles affecting southern pines: A review of current knowledge. S. Forest Exp. Sta., U. S. Forest Serv., Occas. Pap. 180. 25 p.

Vité, J. P., and G. B. Pitman. 1968. Bark beetle aggregation: Effects of feeding on the release of pheromones in *Dendroctonus* and *Ips.* Nature 218: 169–70.

Vité, J. P., and J. A. Renwick. 1968. Insect and host factors in the aggregation of the southern pine beetle. Contrib. Boyce Thompson Inst. 24: 61–63.

Yu, C. C., and C. H. Tsao. 1967. Gallery construction and sexual behavior in the southern pine beetle, *Dendroctonus frontalis* Zimmerman. J. Ga. Entomol. Soc. 2: 95–98.

SEX PHEROMONE PRODUCTION AND REPRODUCTIVE BEHAVIOUR IN GAMMA-IRRADIATED *TENEBRIO MOLITOR*

MAYA MENON and K. K. NAIR

Abstract—Studies to determine the effects of gamma-radiation on sex pheromone production in female *Tenebrio molitor* showed that irradiation of females either as newly emerged or as pharate adults with 3·5 or 7 krad had no significant effect on their sex pheromone activity when compared to that of normals. However, treatment of irradiated insects with a juvenile hormone analogue increased their pheromone activity, whereas it decreased the pheromone activity in the normals.

Ovary maturation was inhibited in irradiated insects, and it could not be alleviated by treatment with juvenile hormone analogue. Since ovarian transplants from normal to irradiated insects showed yolk deposition, whereas reciprocal transplants did not, it is concluded that the inhibition in yolk deposition in the ovaries of irradiated insects was due to radiation damage to the ovary itself rather than to the neuroendocrine system.

Irradiation of the males with 7 krad did not affect their ability to respond to the female sex pheromone or their sexual vigour. At higher doses their response was slow and it decreased with increase in radiation dose, and also as a function of time after irradiation.

INTRODUCTION

IN RECENT years evidence has accumulated in favour of the existence, in most groups of insects, of a sex pheromone which plays a significant rôle in bringing the two sexes together for reproduction (BEROZA, 1970; WOOD *et al.*, 1970). Therefore, sterilizing insect pests for control can be successful only if sterilizing techniques do not interfere with (1) the production of their sex pheromone, (2) their ability to perceive the pheromone, and (3) their normal behaviour. The only studies to date on the above aspects are on the American cockroach, *Periplaneta americana* (WHARTON and WHARTON, 1957), the gypsy moth, *Porthetria dispar* (STATLER, 1970), and the codling moth, *Laspeyresia pomonella* (WHITE and HUTT, 1971). We have investigated in the beetle *Tenebrio molitor*: (1) the effects of gamma-radiation on sex pheromone production and reproductive physiology of the females, (2) the ability of irradiated males to perceive the female sex pheromone, and (3) the sexual vigour of irradiated males. We chose this insect because its pheromone history (VALENTINE, 1931; TSCHINKEL *et al.*, 1967; Tschinkel, 1970; HAPP, 1969,

1970; HAPP and WHEELER, 1969, MENON, 1970; AUGUST, 1971) and reproductive physiology (MORDUE, 1965, 1967; LAVERDURE, 1967; MENON, 1970) are well documented. Since implantation of active larval corpora allata into allatectomized female *T. molitor* promoted yolk deposition (LAVERDURE, 1967) and since topical application of a juvenile hormone (J.H.) analogue induced sex pheromone production in a decapitated female *T. molitor* (MENON, 1970), we also investigated the influence of J.H. on the above aspects in gamma-irradiated *T. molitor*.

MATERIALS AND METHODS

A stock colony was maintained as described by MENON (1970). Pupae were collected, sexed, and held separately in two incubators at 25°C and 12 hr photoperiod. The insects were used to study: (1) bioassay of pheromone of females exposed to gamma-radiation and J.H. treatment, (2) ovarian development in females exposed to gamma-radiation and J.H. treatment, (3) ovarian transplants from normal into irradiated females and vice versa, (4) sensitivity of irradiated males to pheromone extracts of normal females, and (5) assessment of sexual vigour of irradiated males.

Irradiation of females

The insects were irradiated in a ^{60}Co gamma source (Gamma Cell 200, A.E.C.L.) at a dose rate of 1·2 krad/min, measured in air with a Victoreen dosimeter. Newly emerged females were exposed to 3·5 and 7 krad and pharate adults, 1 day before ecdysis, to 7 krad of gamma-radiation. Irradiated and control insects were kept in groups of 5 to 10 in plastic Petri dishes lined with filter paper and provided with bran and water.

Hormone treatment

The J.H. analogue used was *trans-trans*-N,N-diethyl-3,7,11-trimethyl-10,11-epoxydodeca-2,6-dienamide (Syntex), made up in acetone. One to 2 days after adult emergence about 50 per cent of the insects irradiated with 7 krad as pharate adults and 50 per cent of the unirradiated controls were treated with 2 μg of J.H. in acetone by topical application on the mesothorax with disposable micropipettes. The other 50 per cent of the two groups of insects received 2 μl of acetone only and these served as controls.

Pheromone assay

Ten days after adult emergence the control and the irradiated insects, with or without the J.H. treatment, were extracted individually in tetrahydrofuran (1 insect/ml) as described by MENON (1970). Each extract was then tested for biological activity using 20 males by the assay method of TSHINKEL *et al.* (1967).

Estimation of ovary maturation

After extraction of the pheromone the insects were preserved in 70% ethanol. They were dissected and the number of insects with mature ovaries, the number of eggs per insect, and the number of eggs per insect with mature ovaries were determined.

Ovary transplantation

Ovaries of 1- to 2-day-old adult females were transplanted into females of the same age group. Transplantations were made from (1) normal to normal, (2) normal to irradiated (7 krad), and (3) irradiated to normal. Only females irradiated as pharate adults were used. Ovaries with ducts were excised from donor insects and placed in *Tenebrio* saline (BELTON and GRUNDFEST, 1962). The recipient insects were anaesthetized for 1 hr in water through which carbon dioxide bubbled continuously. Then they were affixed on their dorsum in a Petri dish by a strip of Plasticine. Under a binocular microscope a small rectangular incision was made on the ventral side of the eighth abdominal segment, a piece of fat body was removed, and a single ovary from the saline was inserted into the body cavity. The cuticular flap was replaced, surface sterilized with chloremphenicol, dried with cotton wool, and sealed with melted paraffin wax. The recipient insects were returned to the incubators and provided with bran and water 1 day after the operation. After 10 days they were sacrificed and the terminal oöcytes of the transplants were examined for yolk deposition.

Irradiation of males

Insects were collected at random from a month-old population of males and were divided into four groups of 60 each. One group was kept as control and the other three groups were exposed to 7, 16, or 32 krad of gamma-radiation. The sensitivity of these males to pheromone extracts of normal females was tested on days 1, 3, and 6 after irradiation. Furthermore, the sexual vigour of these irradiated males was assessed on day 7 by using combinations involving normal females, normal males, and irradiated males. Three marked males (one normal, one exposed to krad, and the other to 16 krad) per female were confined under a Petri dish for 10 min and their order of mating was observed. Thirty tests were made using 90 males and 30 females.

Statistical analyses

One way analysis of variance and the *t*-test were used to test the significance of differences in pheromone activity in the various groups after different treatments. The data on ovary maturation and on the males' sensitivity to pheromone extracts of females were analysed by the exact hypergeometric one-tail test using LIEBERMAN and OWEN's (1961) tables. The data on males' sexual vigour was analysed by the exact Wilcoxon one-tail test using the above tables. In all tests the minimum significance level was set at $P < 0.05$.

RESULTS

Mortality

Adult mortality was about 15 per cent in the irradiated females and 5 per cent in the controls, up to day 10. Seventy per cent of the normals with ovary transplants and 58 per cent of the irradiated females with ovary transplants survived during the experimental period of 10 days. Exposure of mature males to 16 and 32 krad increased the mortality to 10 and 90 per cent respectively within 8 days of irradiation.

Pheromone activity

Exposure of newly emerged females to 3·5 and 7 krad and pharate adults to 7 krad did not significantly alter their pheromone activity up to 10 days (Table 1). However, application of J.H. to females irradiated with 7 krad increased the pheromone activity significantly above that of controls. On the other hand, treatment of unirradiated females with J.H. decreased their pheromone activity significantly below that of control insects.

TABLE 1—PHEROMONE ACTIVITY OF EXTRACTS OF FEMALE *T. molitor* 10 DAYS AFTER EMERGENCE AND VARIOUS TREATMENTS

Treatment	No. of female extracts tested	Percentage of males responded (mean ± S.E.)	Comparison of means
Newly emerged adults			
1. Unirradiated (controls)	8	52·50 ± 3·85	1 vs. 2, N.S.* 1 vs. 3, N.S.
2. Irradiated (3·5 krad)	5	48·00 ± 6·26	2 vs. 3, N.S.
3. Irradiated (7 krad)	7	55·70 ± 4·87	
Pharate adults			
4. Unirradiated, treated with 2 μl of acetone (controls)	35	51·70 ± 2·68	4 vs. 5, $P < 0.025$ 4 vs. 6, N.S. 4 vs. 7, $P < 0.005$ 5 vs. 6, $P < 0.025$
5. Unirradiated, treated with 2 μg of J.H.	25	39·20 ± 4·08	5 vs. 7, $P < 0.001$ 6 vs. 7, N.S.
6. Irradiated (7 krad), treated with 2 μl of acetone	21	57·20 ± 3·50	
7. Irradiated (7 krad), treated with 2 μg of J.H.	27	62·77 ± 2·97	

* Not significant ($P > 0.05$).

Ovary maturation

Irradiation of newly emerged females with 3·5 krad significantly reduced the number of insects with mature ovaries. However, the number of eggs per insect

169

with mature ovaries was not significantly different from that of the controls. A dose of 7 kR significantly reduced not only the number of insects with mature ovaries but also the number of eggs per insect with mature ovaries, irrespective of whether the insects were irradiated as newly emerged or as pharate adults. Treatment of irradiated insects with J.H. did not repair the inhibition in yolk deposition, whereas J.H. treated controls showed a slight, but not significant ($P = 0.07$), increase in the number of eggs per insect (Table 2).

TABLE 2—EFFECT OF GAMMA-RADIATION AND J.H. APPLICATION ON OVARY MATURATION IN *T. molitor*

Treatment	No. of insects examined	Percentage of insects with mature ovaries	Total No. of eggs	Mean No. of eggs/insect with mature ovaries	Mean No. of eggs/insect
Newly emerged adults					
1. Controls (normal)	68	96a	700	10·9a	10·2a
2. Controls, treated with 2 μg of J.H.	22	95a	281	13·4a	12·8a
3. Irradiated (3·5 krad)	17	71b	81	6·8a	4·8b
4. Irradiated (7 krad)	27	26c	33	4·7c	1·2c
Pharate adults					
5. Irradiated (7 krad)	34	15c	11	2·2c	0·3c
6. Irradiated (7 krad), treated with 2 μg of J.H.	23	15c	10	3·3c	0·4c

Means in the same column followed by the same italic letter are not significantly different at the 5 per cent level of probability.

Ovary transplants

Young ovarian transplants from normal to normal and from normal to irradiated females showed conspicuous yolk deposition 10 days after transplantation, whereas transplants from irradiated to normal females did not (Table 3).

TABLE 3—RESULTS OF TRANSPLANTS OF NORMAL AND IRRADIATED (7 krad) OVARIES INTO NORMAL AND IRRADIATED (7 krad) FEMALE *T. molitor*

Treatment	No. of insects	Survived (%)	Percentage with yolk laden transplants	Comparison of means
1. Normal to normal	11	77	90	1 vs. 2, N.S.*
2. Normal to irradiated	32	58	55	2 vs. 3, $P < 0.005$
3. Irradiated to normal	25	70	0	1 vs. 3, $P < 0.005$

* Not significant ($P > 0.05$).

170

Sensitivity of irradiated males to female pheromone extract

The sensitivity of males exposed to 7 krad was not significantly different from that of control insects on all the 3 days tested. Males irradiated with 16 krad showed a slight decrease in their sensitivity to female extracts 6 days after irradiation, and those exposed to 32 krad did significantly less than those of the other three groups on all the three days tested (Table 4).

TABLE 4—RESPONSE OF IRRADIATED MALE *T. molitor* TO EXTRACTS OF FEMALE SEX PHEROMONE

Group No.	Radiation dose (krad)	No. of insects tested	Percentage of males responded		
			Day 1	Day 3	Day 6
1	0 (controls)	40	67·5	85·0	75·0
2	7	40	85·5	87·5	92·5
3	16	40	85·0	70·0	57·0
4	32	40	55·0	52·5	35·0

Group 1 vs. 2, not significant; 1 vs. 3, not significant; 1 vs. 4, $P < 0·05$ on all days tested; 2 vs. 3, not significant; 2 vs. 4, $P < 0·05$; 3 vs. 4, $P < 0·05$.

Sexual vigour of irradiated males

There was no significant difference in the mating ability of normal males or of those exposed to 7 krad of gamma-radiation. However, the mating ability of males exposed to 16 krad was significantly inhibited (Table 5).

TABLE 5—MATING COMPETITIVENESS OF MALE *T. molitor* 7 DAYS AFTER IRRADIATION

Rank	Normal	7 krad	16 krad
Percentage of males mated first	33·3	46·0	6·6
Percentage of males mated second	45·0	18·8	10·7
Percentage of males mated third	0	15·4	16·7
Percentage of males mated from each group	78·3	80·2	34·0

Normal vs. 7 krad, N.S.
Normal vs. 16 krad, $P < 0·05$.
Seven krad vs. 16 krad, $P < 0·05$.

DISCUSSION

Our data show that doses of gamma-radiation that inhibit yolk deposition do not interfere with sex pheromone production in female *T. molitor*. This is in conformity with STATLER's (1970) observations from field studies that radiation sterilization of female gypsy moth, *P. dispar*, does not affect its attractiveness to males. WHARTON and WHARTON (1957) showed that in *P. americana* low doses of 2 MeV electrons damaged oöthecal production permanently and pheromone production temporarily, but on recovery the pheromone production overshot the normal level. Since there is an inverse relationship between oöthecal production and pheromone production, WHARTON and WHARTON concluded that the increase in pheromone production was due to the destruction by irradiation of the mechanism associated with oöthecal production. Whether this is due to radiation damage to the colleterial glands, ovaries, or via damage to the neuroendocrine system is not evident from their studies. Although the role of J.H. in yolk deposition in insects is established (ENGELMANN, 1970), the inhibition of yolk deposition observed in the irradiated *T. molitor* was not alleviated by external application of J.H. It is also known that J.H. is involved in the production of sex pheromone in the cockroach, *Byrsotria fumigata* (EMMERICH and BARTH. 1968), the bark beetle, *Ips paraconfusus (confusus)* (BORDEN *et al.*, 1969), and in *T. molitor* (MENON, 1970). Therefore, if the pheromone synthesizing mechanism is not damaged by irradiation, the excess of J.H. applied to the insect may be utilized by it to increase pheromone production. This perhaps accounts for the higher level of pheromone activity in the irradiated *T. molitor* treated with J.H. On the contrary, normal females treated with J.H. showed a decrease in pheromone level on day 10. It is likely that the excess of J.H. triggers the mechanism of yolk deposition, which in some manner inhibits the mechanism of pheromone production. BELL and BARTH (1970) have demonstrated this inverse relationship between yolk deposition and pheromone production in *B. fumigata* that have been treated with excess of J.H.

The ovaries of irradiated *T. molitor* failed to mature either in the presence of J.H. or after their transplantation into normal females, whereas irradiated beetles deposited yolk in ovarian transplants from normal insects. Hence, there is strong inference that the inhibition in yolk deposition in the ovaries of irradiated insects is due to radiation damage to the ovary itself rather than to the neuroendocrine system. BAILEY and SHIPP (1970) came to similar conclusions using irradiated *Dacus cucumis*. According to LA CHANCE and BURNS (1963) the inhibition in yolk deposition in irradiated *Cochliomyia hominivorax* was due to damage to the nurse cells. In the case of the *T. molitor*, however, it is not certain whether the radiation damage is to the nurse cells and/or to the follicle cells.

Radiation sensitivity of the various developmental stages of *T. molitor* have been reported (NICHOLAS and WIANT, 1959; MENHINICK and CROSSLEY, 1968) but little is known of the effect of radiation on the induction of sterility in males or their ability to perceive sex pheromone after exposure to radiation. Some preliminary observations indicated that 7 krad is a substerilizing dose, whereas 16 krad induces 99·9 per cent sterility in the males of *T. molitor*. Although irradiation of males with 7 and 16 krad did not impair their ability to perceive the pheromone from female extracts, their mating competitiveness (sexual vigour) was severely affected at 16 krad. It is pertinent to mention here that WHITE and HUTT (1971) found that when males of *L. pomonella* were irradiated with various doses of gamma-radiation and released in a field, the number of irradiated males caught in traps baited with females decreased with increase in radiation dose. This has been attributed to loss in vigour in irradiated insects. In our studies we observed that most of the males irradiated with 16 kR were lethargic within 7 days of irradiation. Whether this was due to structural damage to the sarcoplasmic reticulum and mitochondria of the skeletal muscles similar to that observed in the flight muscles of gamma-irradiated housefly *Musca domestica* (NAIR and BHAKTHAN, 1969) is currently being investigated.

Acknowledgements—The research was supported by National Research Council of Canada grants A 4669 and E 1538 awarded to Dr. K. K. NAIR. We thank Dr. J. B. SIDDALL of Zoecon for the generous gift of the J.H. analogue, Dr. M. CREIG for assistance in the statistical analyses, Drs. J. H. BORDEN and J. M. WEBSTER for constructive criticism of the manuscript, and Mr. B. DEAN for maintenance of the insect colony.

REFERENCES

AUGUST C. J. (1971) The rôle of male and female pheromone in the mating behaviour of *Tenebrio molitor*. *J. Insect Physiol.* **17**, 739–752.

BAILEY P. and SHIPP E. (1970) Corpus allatum size and ovarian environment in irradiated cucumber fly, *Dacus cucumis*. *J. Insect Physiol.* **16**, 1293–1299.

BELL W. J. and BARTH R. H., (1970) Quantitative effects of juvenile hormone on reproduction in the cockroach *Byrsotria fumigata*. *J. Insect Physiol.* **16**, 2303–2313.

BELTON P. B. and GRUNDFEST H. (1962) Potassium activation and K spikes in muscle fibers of the mealworm larva (*Tenebrio molitor*). *Am. J. Physiol.* **203**, 588–594.

BEROZA M. (1970) *Chemicals Controlling Insect Behaviour*. Academic Press, New York.

BORDEN J. H., NAIR K. K., and SLATER C. E. (1969) Synthetic juvenile hormone: induction of sex pheromone production in *Ips confusus*. *Science, Wash.* **166**, 1626–1627.

EMMERICH H. and BARTH R. H., JR. (1968) Effect of farnesyl methyl ether on reproductive physiology in the cockroach, *Byrsotria fumigata* (Guérin). *Z. Naturf.* **23b**, 1019–1020.

ENGELMANN F. (1970) *The Physiology of Insect Reproduction*. Pergamon Press, Oxford.

HAPP G. M. (1969) Multiple sex pheromones of the mealworm beetle, *Tenebrio molitor* L. *Nature, Lond.* **222**, 180–181.

HAPP G. M. (1970) Maturation response of male *Tenebrio molitor* to female sex pheromone. *Ann. ent. Soc. Am.* **63**, 1782.

HAPP G. M. and WHEELER J. (1969) Bioassay, preliminary purification, and effect of age, crowding, and mating on the release of sex pheromone by female *Tenebrio molitor*. *Ann. ent. Soc. Am.* **62**, 846–851.

LA CHANCE L. E. and BURNS S. B. (1963) Oogenesis and radiosensitivity in *Cochliomyia hominivorax* (Diptera: Calliphoridae). *Biol. Bull., Woods Hole* **124**, 65–83.

LAVERDURE A. M. (1967) Rôles de l'alimentation et des hormones cérébrales dans la vitellogenèse chez *Tenebrio molitor* (Coléoptère). *Bull. Soc. zool. Fr.* **92**, 629–640.

LIEBERMAN G. J. and OWEN D. B. (1961) *Tables of the Hypergeometric Probability Distribution*. Stanford University Press.

MENHINICK E. F. and CROSSLEY D. A., JR. (1968) A comparison of radiation profiles of *Acheta domesticus* and *Tenebrio molitor*. *Ann. ent. Soc. Am.* **61**, 1359–1365.

MENON M. (1970) Hormone–pheromone relationships in the beetle *Tenebrio molitor*. *J. Insect Physiol.* **16**, 1123–1139.

MORDUE W. (1965) Neuro-endocrine factors in the control of oöcyte production in *Tenebrio molitor* L. *J. Insect Physiol.* **11**, 617–629.

MORDUE W. (1967) The influence of feeding upon the activity of the neuroendocrine system during oöcyte growth in *Tenebrio molitor*. *Gen. comp. Endocr.* **9**, 406–415.

NAIR K. K. and BHAKTHAN N. M. G. (1969) Preliminary studies on the ultrastructural damage in the flight muscles of gamma-irradiated housefly. *Int. J. radiat. Biol.* **16**, 397–399.

NICHOLAS R. C. and WIANT D. E. (1959) Radiation of important grain-infesting pests: order of death curves, and survival values for the various metamorphic forms. *Food Technol.* **13**, 58–62.

STATLER M. W. (1970) Effects of gamma radiation on the ability of the adult female gypsy moth to attract males. *J. econ. Ent.* **63**, 163–164.

TSCHINKEL W. R. (1970) Chemical studies on the sex pheromone of *Tenebrio molitor* (Coleoptera: Tenebrionidae). *Ann. Ent. Soc. Am.* **63**, 626–627.

TSCHINKEL W. R., WILSON C., and BERN H. A. (1967) Sex pheromone of the mealworm beetle, *Tenebrio molitor* L. *J. exp. Zool.* **164**, 81–96.

VALENTINE J. M. (1931) The olfactory sense of the adult mealworm beetle, *Tenebrio molitor* L. *J. exp. Zool.* **58**, 165–227.

WHARTON M. L. and WHARTON D. R. A. (1957) The production of sex attractant substance and of oöthecae by the normal and irradiated American cockroach, *Periplaneta americana* L. *J. Insect Physiol.* **1**, 229–239.

WHITE L. D. and HUTT R. B. (1971) Codling moth catches in sex and light traps after exposure to 0, 25 to 40 krad of gamma irradiation. *J. econ. Ent.* **64**, 1249–1250.

WOOD D. L., SILVERSTEIN R. M., and NAKATIMA M. (1970) *Control of Insect Behavior by Natural Products.* Academic Press, New York.

174

AUTHOR INDEX

KEY-WORD TITLE INDEX